SCHAFFHAUSEN

Rhine

Bischofszell

°Arlesheim

WINTERTHUR

ZURICH

Lake of
Zurich

Aare

Knutwyl

Horgen

Lachen

Lake
Zug

Zug

Einsiedeln

LUCERNE

Arth

Gersau ○SCHWYZ

RNE

Alpnach

Stans

Lake of
Lucerne

Sarnen

Kerns

Klausen Pass

Engelberg

Disentis

Lake
Brienz

Susten Pass

Lake
Jhun

INTERLAKEN

Andermatt

Grimsel
Pass

Jungfrau

Ticino

Lötschental

Reckingen

re Rhone

BRIGUE

Ticino

Glis

BELLINZONA

i s

Saas Balen

Ascona

Lake
Maggiore

LUGANO

Lake
Lugano

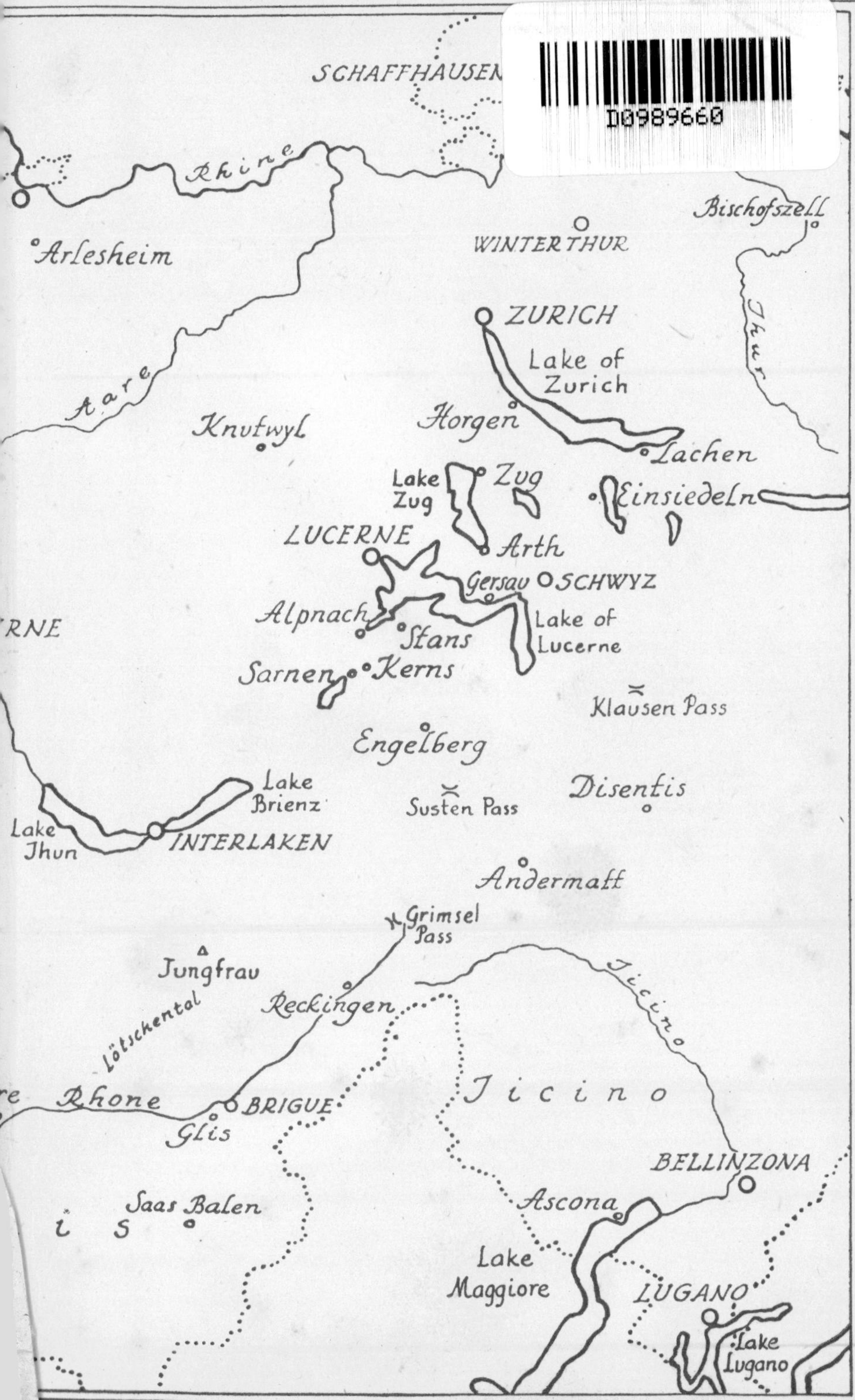

Thomas Beatty Berdeja
801 North Willett
Memphis, Tennessee 38107
(901) 276-5783
Began reading on October 6, 2004
Finished reading on October 8, 2004

SWITZERLAND

BOOKS
ON THE COUNTRIES OF EUROPE

THE LAND OF FRANCE
By Ralph Dutton and Lord Holden

THE LAND OF ITALY
By Jasper More

THE NETHERLANDS
By Sacheverell Sitwell

THE ALPS
By R. L. G. Irving

SPAIN
By Sacheverell Sitwell

In Preparation

BELGIUM AND LUXEMBOURG
By Tudor Edwards

PORTUGAL
By Sacheverell Sitwell

SCANDINAVIA
By Eric de Maré

BATSFORD BOOKS

1   Geneva : La Place du Molard.   *From the painting by R. P. Bonington.*

Reproduced, by permission, from the original in the Victoria and Albert Museum, London

SWITZERLAND

By

John Russell

B. T. BATSFORD LTD

LONDON · NEW YORK
TORONTO · SYDNEY

To
HARRY BATSFORD

First Published, 1950

Made and Printed in Great Britain by Hazell Watson and Viney Ltd
Aylesbury and London for the Publishers
B. T. BATSFORD LTD., LONDON: 15 North Audley Street, W.1 & Malvern Wells
Worcestershire; NEW YORK: 122 East 55th Street; TORONTO: 103 St. Clair Avenue West;
SYDNEY; 156 Castlereagh Street

PREFACE

THIS book is intended rather to supplement than to replace the established guides to Switzerland. It presents the findings of an enthusiast—but an enthusiast of recent date, who cannot rival (and, indeed, does not envy) the monomania of those who speak of Switzerland from the memory of forty or fifty years of annual visits. I have lingered and digressed in my account of the regions with which I happen to be most familiar; and there are many popular resorts with which I have dealt glancingly, or not at all. My excuse must be that, unless one knows everything about everywhere, it is always better to follow where affectionate prejudice is beckoning —and this nowhere more so than in Switzerland, where a most intensive tourist activity is combined with almost total neglect of many of the most interesting parts of the country. It is these disregarded areas which I have sought to extol. So far from copying the fastidiousness of those who pass through Switzerland with averted eye, I have at times allowed myself to go to the contrary extreme; and when in doubt I have generally turned for counsel to the maxim of Vauvenargues which asserts that "c'est un grand signe de médiocrité que de toujours louer médiocrement."

I should like to acknowledge my debt to Llewellyn Powys' *Swiss Essays* (John Lane, 1947), and C.-F. Ramuz' *Vues Sur Le Valais* (Urs Graf, Basle) from both of which I have pillaged as largely as I dared; to the Notebooks of Gerard Manley Hopkins (Oxford, 1937); and above all to Dr. Jenny's *Kunstführer der Schweiz* (Buchler & Co., Berne)—the most complete, intelligent and luminous architectural guide ever published, in pocket size, about any European country.

Mr. Elliot Felkin has been kind enough to lend me the fruit of his many years' study of Genevan history; and for other kindnesses

I am indebted to Professor H. W. Haüsermann and Mr. Michael Sadleir.

Parts of Chapter One have appeared in the *Cornhill Magazine* and *The New Statesman and Nation*, and I am grateful to the Editors of these two journals for permission to reprint.

I am most grateful also to Doctor H. R. Conrad for the many useful suggestions he made after reading the book in proof.

J. R.

JANUARY 1950

CONTENTS

ACKNOWLEDGMENT

The Author and Publishers here express their indebtedness to the following persons and institutions for the illustrations mentioned:

L. Beringer, Zürich, for Fig. 54; Gh. Dubost, Crans (Valais), for Fig. 50; Edit. de l'Ass. Pro Abbatiale, Payerne, for Fig. 37; the Exclusive News Agency, London, for Figs. 12, 25, 55 and 62; Foto Kino Gross, St. Gallen, for Fig. 10; Jules Geiger, Flims-Waldhaus, for Fig. 82; P. Heman, Basel, for Fig. 36; G. Wren Howard, Esq., for Fig. 20; Keystone Press Agency, Ltd., for Fig. 4; Literary Services (Mondiale) Ltd., for Figs. 5, 6 and 70; The National Library, Berne, for Figs. 16 and 22; Foto Poncaldi, Ascona, for Fig. 76; Messrs. Paul Popper, London, for Figs. 8, 9, 13, 14, 26, 39, 57, 65, 69, 75, 77, 80 and 81; A. Sartori, Lausanne, for Fig. 19; Theodor Geiger, Basel, for Figs. 2, 3, 7, 23, 31, 32, 34, 35, 40, 47, 56, 58, 59, 60, 61, 68, 84, 85, 86, 89, 90, 91, 92, 93, 94 and 96; Steinemann, Locarno, for Figs. 48 and 71; The Swiss Federal Railways and National Tourist Office, London, for Figs. 11, 15, 17, 18, 24, 27, 28, 29, 30, 33, 38, 41, 42, 43, 46, 48, 50, 51, 52, 53, 54, 63, 64, 66, 71, 72, 73, 74, 79, 83, 87 and 95; Messrs. Topical Press Agency, Ltd., London, for Figs. 44, 45 and 78; Verlag Huber, Frauenfeld, for Figs. 2, 7, 59, 67, 68 and 91; the Victoria and Albert Museum, London, and The Medici Society, for Fig. 1; and Wehrli, Zürich, for Fig. 88.

They would also like to thank Dr. Hans Zbinden for having obtained photographs of the two prints in the National Library, Berne.

The jacket, of Lucerne, is reproduced from a French lithograph of *circa* 1845. The Publishers are most grateful to Messrs. W. T. Spencer, of New Oxford Street, for loaning the original.

2 Sculpture on the west façade of the Abbey Church (1763-4; *after J. A. Feuchtmayr*) (*left*)

3 Stucco decoration on the Kleine Engelberg, Marktgasse (*c.* 1750) (*right*)

ST. GALL

4   Alpine pinnacles above Val Bregaglia

INTRODUCTION

HARDY and nosy, flannelled and rosy, the English tourist has been for many years a familiar apparition upon the European scene. Though most variously interpreted by foreign observers, he is really of ingenuous, enduring metal. His habits do not change; at most they suffer some variation of scale and place. There may not be such a crush round the bandstand at Wiesbaden, and if Trollope were rewriting *Phineas Redux*, he would no longer send Lady Laura to repine at Koenigstein. If Mr. Gladstone, again, were to appear, like the Stone Guest, at the Hôtel Carlton, Biarritz, he would find still the tumultuous seas in which he once delighted, and still perhaps the wild strawberries which, consumed in great quantity on December 20th, 1891, caused him to spend the following day in his room; but, whether wraith or stone, he would not find, I fancy, the English huntsmen and the pack of English hounds whose greeting so agreeably surprised him at a later stage in his visit. Such phenomena are the last refinement of favour; fashion, poverty and war have lately narrowed the vision of the English tourist until there is now only one country in which one may be sure of finding many sturdy enclaves of our species. I need not name this country; for even if it were not the subject of this book, it would leap to the reader's mind.

Practised travellers usually think Switzerland rather dull. Except, indeed, for the forbidding and gregarious élite of ski-ers, and the quieter, more solitary masters of alpinism, Swiss travel has no hazards. The timid and the ailing can find in it a greater degree of security than in any other country in the world. Crime exists, but it has not managed to impose itself upon the texture of Swiss society. Perhaps for this reason, the trial of even a minor criminal excites great attention in the elsewhere peaceful pages of the *Journal de Genève* and the *Neue Zürcher Zeitung*; but the poisoners, the incendiaries and the disnatured hairdressers soon give place to local sport and local pieties. A casual visitor could not, in fact, sense their existence; they are merely one of the many disagreeable features of ordinary life which, in Switzerland, do not obtrude. The abnormality of life in all other European countries has lately given an almost preposterous edge to the sedate propriety which rules in these twenty-two cantons. One can live there for a long time without having to face the facts of cruelty, poverty, faction, irremediable disease and open lust.

The Industrial Revolution, though nowhere more important and effective, has also a way of not showing itself; even Winterthur impresses, not as a thriving industrial city, but as the repository of an exemplary Germanic culture. Most visitors make more of the woodcarvers of Brienz than of the Oerlikon factories; and more conspicuous than either is the husbandry to which a vague benison is always attached in the mind of a casual observer. The monuments of Switzerland are also well adapted to the need of invalids or beginners. With few exceptions, they are not of the highest European class. The pilgrim need not fear that lasting congestion of eye and mind which follows a first clamber among the golden debris of Italian civilization; the audacities of the Moors at Valladolid or of Pedro de Ribera at Madrid are reproduced only in polite and diminished form in a country which has known neither the splendid insolence of the great landed proprietor nor the kindred rashness of extravagant belief. The landscape of Switzerland is also perfectly designed for those in whom only extremes of natural grandeur can evoke the notion of the sublime. Such extremes have of course their arduous side; and of this the *British Ski Year-book* will give an authentic and exhilarating account; but this is not a book for mountaineers, and as our more energetic friends step aboard the train for Davos or Zermatt we can only wish them farewell and urge upon them the equipment prescribed by Baedeker—a light *gibecière* or game-bag, a leathern drinking-cup, an opera-glass, a pocket lantern, some lengths of manila hemp and an aneroid barometer. Their pleasures know no change or abatement; and it is for us to find on lower slopes a rival element, if not of risk, at least of surprise. The strenuosities of the slalom and the Cresta Run are, after all, of recent origin; in 1865 the ski itself was unknown in Switzerland and, as Mr. Arnold Lunn has pointed out, would have remained so but for the contagious example of English fanatics. From the simplest beginnings has arisen the most recent of the many metamorphoses which this tiny country has undergone in the eyes of its admirers. In the fifteenth century a paragon of hardihood and military skill, and in the sixteenth the tormented theatre of the Reformers' conscience, Switzerland later became, from the English point of view, successively a precarious refuge for republicans and a convenient and inexpensive rendezvous for travellers *en route* for the grand experience of Italy. Switzerland was, for Gibbon, the unexacting nursemaid of his most testing labours; for Rousseau, the giant barometer of his sensibilities; for Byron also, a sure conductor of violent emotion; and for several generations of Victorian rowing dons, a snowy background to ethical debate. In our own century Lenin, Busoni and Jung have lived in Zürich during

5 A decorated house in the Emmental

6 The village street at Pontresina

7   Arlesheim : the Abbey Church. The west front, rebuilt 1744-5.
Architect, Giovanni Gaspare Bagnato

important periods of their lives; Rilke and James Joyce did much of their best work in Switzerland, and are buried there. The suppression of amenity in the three great surrounding civilizations of France, Germany and Italy has given even the smaller Swiss towns the status of international centres. Schaffhausen (95, 96), for example, is a town of singular architectural merit, and is graced by a curious phenomenon of nature—the cascades of the Rhine; but even so it is surprising to find it named in the *Burlington Magazine* as the temporary custodian of a magnificent exhibition of old German Masters. Paphian beauties from the hand of Maillol extend their marmoreal invitations behind the privet hedges of Winterthur; and Bergson, Jünger, Hölderlin and Malraux enjoy the tasteful extravagance of a Swiss publisher's resources. The puissance of Flagstad's Isolde finds in Geneva its most phlegmatic audience; and in the permanent opera-houses of Basle, Berne and Zürich no novelty is found too forbidding—though even there, perhaps, audiences are best pleased when the elder Germont brings to *Provenza di mar* a voice of softest Angora. If Kleist means little to you or you need to brush up your Grillparzer, these theatres will put you on the right road; and amateurs of oddity will find themselves rewarded by German-Swiss translations of Molière and the Elizabethans. Switzerland is in fact a museum, not merely of plain dealing and normal honesty in human relations, but also of that solid, unexcitable European culture which it was formerly the privilege of Freiburg or Leipzig to offer to young Englishmen in their twenty-second year. How often, in the approved biographies of statesmen and diplomatists, do we not read of the year spent peacefully in some clerical or professorial home, and followed in orthodox fashion by a strenuous term at Scoones'? Bonn and Heidelberg are inaccessible now; the universities of Switzerland, which in the nineteenth century could boast of such great names as Nietzsche and Sainte-Beuve, and of the continuing aura of Erasmus and Rousseau, now preserve the last example of that federated learning which should be the birthright of every European. Swiss museums embrace every sort of human curiosity; there are museums of boots and shoes, museums of railways, museums of mountaineering, museums of fish and museums of cheese. Some drowsy green-shuttered house in a back street of Nyon or Olten will yield always a new proof of this nation's genius for hoarding—a collection of English coins, a two-headed calf preserved in spirit, some citations from the war of 1914–18, a little-known Courbet or a bust by Sarah Bernhardt; and when it comes to a local artist, Hodler and Liotard can count upon limitless room, while in the Kunsthaus at Zürich, Fuseli, most disturbing of painters, scampers across the centuries in search of phantom-subjects from

3

Milton and Ben Jonson, or blandly proffers his own inmost images of disquiet.

Switzerland is solid for culture—solid, that is to say, for the unexcited appreciation of everything that is generally accepted as good. Pascal and Dante occupy columns in the morning papers; Mr. Charles Morgan's lectures, no less than the restrained Byronism of his personal appearance, make a gratifyingly solid impression. Living artists must rely upon individuals for patronage; Stravinsky and James Joyce, for example, did not receive much support, during their stay in Switzerland, from those quarters which will canonize them in 1975. The dead are surest of their welcome. For them no trouble will be too great. For them the wealth of Switzerland will be spent freely. This wealth should never be discounted by any appreciative traveller, for it is behind many of his pleasures. Nature herself profits by it, and it serves to keep the creations of man in exemplary trim. How many baroque monuments are in as good condition as Einsiedeln and Arlesheim? Where else in Europe could one find the spangled and glistening polish of such towns as Diessenhofen and Stein-am-Rhein? The Valais is poor country, technically speaking; but even there one has not the sensation of indigence which similar regions in France or Italy are only too well able to inspire. Where money is concerned, the Swiss have always been at once discreet and tough. Rousseau describes, in a passage of almost allegorical interest, how once in the neighbourhood of Motiers, "I sat down on a cushion of moss and lycopodium and gave myself over to daydreams, in the knowledge that I had found a refuge unknown to anyone else, and where my persecutors could not run me to earth. While I was enjoying this sensation I heard, a little way below, a certain familiar clicking. The noise came again and again until, in surprise and anxiety, I forced my way through a thicket of brushwood in the direction of the sound, and discovered that stockings were being made in a little hollow not twenty yards from where I had thought myself a pioneer explorer."

In nearly every Swiss town there is that sense of comfort and careful well-being which is induced by fresh paint, well-tended woodwork, painted eaves and gilded fountains erect among a scarlet foliage of geraniums. Luxury is often vulgar in Switzerland, as it is everywhere; but the villas above Lugano and the temples of opulence along the Zürichsee count for little in the ensemble of Swiss life. It would be fairer to point out that only one in every hundred Swiss houses is without electric light, and that central heating has existed in this country since 1840. Wealth crops up suddenly in Switzerland, and the result may be either a whole town—like the watchmaking township of La Chaux-de-Fonds, run up in a generation at a height of 3,000 feet among the bare limestone hills of the Jura—or a great mansion like the Stockalper Palace, which disputes with the Jesuitenkirche (itself largely the creation of the Stockalper family) for the domination of Brigue (41). All those who have travelled across the Simplon Pass will remember this palace which, as an example of individual fantasy and family pride, has few equals in Switzerland; even the earthquake of 1755 could not destroy it, and it has stood for three centuries to give southbound travellers their first whiff of the Italian style. Its towers and gilded cupolas are an example, rare in Switzerland, of flaunted riches; it is more common for wealth to call quietly to wealth among the discreet mansions of the Rittergasse at Basle. For a cosmopolitan minority, wealth is a matter of prudent investment in such Swiss concerns as are based in South America; but the mere tourist (and who can disdain a name hallowed by Stendhal?) will not normally go so deep. For him, Switzerland may well seem an unblemished paradise—the earthly double, indeed, of that promised garden of Mahomet, in which abounded "umbrageous groves, fountains and black-eyed girls".

This garden has of course been very thoroughly explored by English travellers. The first testimony in Professor de Beer's recent anthology is dated 990; and in the last two centuries books about Switzerland have been beyond computation. Few of them are other than rhapsodical in their terms. We English are, in spite of appearances, a full-hearted people, and in our enjoyment of Swiss scenery we have spoken from inner reserves of emotion which even the speakers themselves might have rejected, in any other context, as fulsome and absurd. "The Alps were for Stephen a playground, but they were also a cathedral." What was said of Sir Leslie Stephen could be said of all the great preachers (for that is their true name) who have followed him. Himself a professed agnostic, Stephen was one of those men whose withdrawal from organized religion serves only to exacerbate their craving to believe; but in the worship of mountains, believer and disbeliever are one. Mr. Arnold Lunn's position is remote from that of those who accepted *An Agnostic's Apology*; but from his books, as from those of Mr. R. L. G. Irving, one may gauge how strong, beyond all counterfeit, is the real, the evangelical passion of the mountain-lover. When Mr. Irving writes, "It is my one regret for being just an ordinary man, that I bring so little credit to the mountains that have done so much for me", it is impossible not to respect and admire the strength of his impulse. When Mr. Lunn writes, "The hills stand round Jerusalem, and the great Alps still tower above the tormented plains, and in their

unshrinking splendour still bear witness to the eternal loveliness which
man cannot mar and time cannot corrupt", it is possible to demur,
but again impossible to deny the evidence of Mr. Lunn's passion,
which at this moment is celebrating its jubilee. These feelings are so
strong as to brook no opposition. (Tennyson, for instance, has never
been forgiven for his "I was satisfied with the size of crags, but
mountains, great mountains, disappointed me".) Yet there is room
for a book in English about ground-level Switzerland. The two
volumes of Beattie, the three volumes of Coxe, are not inspiriting. In
our own tongue the alpinists are easy winners, but in French and
German this is not so. The more highly developed consciousness (in
certain respects) of these two races has given them a more critical
outlook. There are men, and great men at that, who have detested
the Alps. Flaubert was one of them. "I would give all the glaciers",
he wrote, "for the Vatican Museum . . . the Alps are too big to be
any use to us." But in England only the minute and deleterious art
of Ronald Firbank has opposed itself to the Eleusinian ramblings of
the other side. "Mountains can never be high enough for me," he
pipes; "I should like to *shake* Switzerland."

The ski-er and the mountaineer are naturally devoted to the landscape which provides them with their hardy enjoyments; and there
are some types of contemplative person whose minds work more
freely and more easily among mountain scenery. Mountains intensify
whatever thoughts they may have at the time. As they moulder
happily in front of the Weisshorn or the Wengernalp, their mental
procedures take on the mirage of a rival immensity. The Alps serve
every point of view. To-day the image of a peace elsewhere denied
to us, they represented for Wordsworth a call to battle. "The fife
of war", he wrote:

> *"Was then a spirit-stirring sound indeed,*
> *A blackbird's whistle in a budding grove."*

Mountains, like dogs, assume the outlook of those who love them.

For myself, I find the works of man quite as inspiring as the works
of nature, and I think it a pity that this curious and remarkable
country should be so much associated with the trivial pantheism of
its Victorian admirers. The Swiss themselves have not been so exclusive. Lifelong familiarity with these mountains has led them to
put as high a value upon other attributes of their country. Even
their fantasies differ from those of the *Alpine Journal*. Alexandre
Cingria, for example, reverted for preference to a primitive age in
which, for a few months every year, the waterside villages between

8　A Cemetery of the Bündner Oberland

9　A Christmas Service near Davos

11 Morcote : the Madonna del Sasso

10 Diessenhofen : the Clock Tower (1545)

Bienne and Neuchâtel bore the aspect of a northern Polynesia and personages of ideal beauty lay naked in the sunshine or slipped like porpoises through tepid and waveless waters. Dr. Peter Meyer's visions are more practical; but there is something to set the mind alight in his allusion to the Greek vase of the sixth century B.C. which was discovered near Berne, and to the fact that five hundred years later Cæsar reported that the army registers of the Helvetiæ were still written in Greek characters. One does not need to be a scholar to be touched by the solitary Roman column at Avenches, or by that golden head of an Antonine Emperor which is the prime relic of the sunken and dismembered city of Aventicum. In the treasury of St. Maurice the objects may not all satisfy the most exacting æsthetic taste, but this collection, crowded as it is with the accretions of twelve centuries of pilgrimage, outmasters all the trophies of the saleroom. Only the dullest visitor could fail to take fire from the succession of nicely graded habitations which leads from the rude stone hutches at the summit of the Klausen pass to the Romanesque masterpieces at Payerne (37) and Chur (83), the Burgundian châteaux in the Pays de Vaud, the exemplary town-houses of Rorschach and Zug, the painted eaves of Fribourg and Schwarzenburg, the numberless timber farmsteads of the German-speaking cantons, and such splendid aggregates as the waterfront of Basle (88, 90), the Limmatquai at Zürich (53), and the entire village of Morcote (11) in the Tessin. There is so much, in Switzerland, to please and excite the eye. This country makes convalescents of us all; without challenging us to the supreme effort demanded by Mansard or Bernini, it encourages in every writer an unresisting euphoria; and it is something of this which I shall try to convey.

Much must depend upon one's point of vantage. Distance in space lent enchantment even to Gibbon's view of Lausanne. Distance in time, on the other hand, may occasion discouraging failures of knowledge and sympathy. Archdeacon Coxe, writing in the year of the French Revolution, enquired whether anyone, "in the least conversant in letters, is unacquainted with the celebrated names of Oecolampadius, Amerbach, the three Bauhins, Grynaeus, Buxtorf, Wetstein, Iselin. . . ." I dare to hope that many of my readers will be as ignorant of these figures as I was myself, until I looked them up in the dictionary. Time and place must be allowed for; how else should we understand our forbears? Coxe himself, writing in the shelving garden at Bemerton, where once George Herbert had walked in sight of Salisbury spire, was a Whig historian, a Fellow of King's and an astute collector of livings; a miscellaneous writer, the chronicler of the Austrian and Spanish monarchies and the

administrations of Pelham; if not the biographer, at any rate the por-
traitist, of Correggio, Parmegiano and Handel. Dr. William Beattie
was nearly fifty years younger than the Archdeacon, and in his capacity
as physician to King William IV (then the Duke of Clarence) he had
on three occasions accompanied the Royal Duke on a tour of the
Courts of Germany. These peaceful and opulent journeys supply the
element of animation which, in spite of his intimacy with Lady
Blessington, Lady Byron, Thomas Campbell and Samuel Rogers,
would seem to have been denied to Dr. Beattie in his private capacity.
As a member of the Royal Household he could compile at any rate
the chapter-headings for a book of exceptional charm. "The Royal
Bath," we read, "St. Vitus' Waltz—Remark of a Lady—Trans-
parencies, Devices—Unpleasant Apprehensions—Visit to the Aeolian
Harp." The narrative does not gratify the hopes thus subtly aroused;
nor do such merely cryptic headings as "Hawk—Opitz—Maxim—
Stone Doors—Spaniel" repay investigation. Beattie, like Coxe, is
dull. It would be invidious, and at times impertinent, to scrutinize
later writers in the same fashion. I have inserted in the text my
acknowledgments to the many enthusiasts and the few men of genius
from whose works I have presumed to enlarge my small stocks of
knowledge and assurance. My own theodolite has been set up in a
district which has no affinity with Switzerland, and yet is mentioned
in a once-famous creation of the Swiss imagination. The book in
question is now little read. A reader of genius, and the author of that
sagacious maxim, "They say life is the thing, but I prefer reading",
once felt bound to refute Hazlitt by saying, "Alas! we might sit in a
field for ever with *Julie* open before us, but we couldn't read it".
Rousseau's novel is as long as the complete Whitaker, and much
less amusing; but towards the middle of it Mylord Edouard Bomston
returns to England. Unaccountably he lingers at "Kinsington", where
the Court was then established. Great is the agitation of the narrator,
and boundless her suspicions! It is in this same beguiling "Kinsington" that I first set up my little observatory.

12   Mürren, with the Eiger and Mönch

13   Edelweiss in the Upper Engadine

The range of the Bernese Alps seen from the Jura eighty-five miles away

I

Geneva and the Pays de Vaud

Geneva—Lac Léman—Lausanne—Vevey—Montreux

SWITZERLAND can be taken by siege or by storm. Both methods have their merits. Mountain country can advantageously be approached by air; and whereas, for example, the matchless hinterland of France can only be seen properly at ground-level, the outline of the Oberland must evoke a start of excitement even among those who happen to be a mile higher than its topmost peaks (14). Things seen from a great height acquire the impersonal air of classical landscape; altitude, as surely as three centuries of dirt and varnish, reduces the incurious ploughman and his team to the stature of figures in a Koninck or a Cuyp; and this aptly introduces us to a landscape so often admired for its supposed power to suppress all sense of human personality. As the aeroplane shaves the apple-green uplands of the Jura, therefore, and we see it reflected for a moment in high-lying pools or spreading its shadow across three acres of inaccessible pasture, there is time to brace ourselves for the ordeal of the Alps. Those who fly to Switzerland may find it less agreeable to travel than to arrive; the wonder of the intermediary landscape is lost, but the wonder of Switzerland, and the strangeness, are enhanced.

There are many possible overland routes, and none which does not progressively arouse one's curiosity about this country, the abrupt and ornamental centre of Europe. Coasting through the mud-flats of the Lombard plain and skirting the filthy hump of Domodossola, the mind naturally forms for itself visions of a more agreeable landscape, and this the first stretch of the Simplon, with its darkening gorges, concealed waterfall and Napoleonic chophouse, has no difficulty in providing. The blank and torpid towns of the German Rhineland, again, cannot now hope to rival the healthy complacence of life in Basle. But most English visitors will arrive from France, and on that road they will have met with unsurpassable enjoyments. Even before they embark at Newhaven, the valley of the Ouse, green-shouldered and patched with chalk, will tempt them to stay at home. At Dieppe, while drunken longshoremen fight patiently for their equilibrium beneath Sickert's arcades, they will note how the war has given to the façade of St. Ouen that same silvery roughness which this painter had bestowed upon it some thirty years earlier. Once out among the green and yellow prairies of Normandy, the opening paragraph of *Lamiel* may come to mind. "People praise Switzerland highly," Stendhal wrote; "but one has to buy its mountains at the cost of three days of boredom, the annoyances of the customs-house and a passport stuffed with visas. Whereas one has only to enter Normandy for the eye, weary of the symmetries of Paris and its white walls, to be welcomed by an ocean of verdure." From the air this ocean becomes polite geometry; from eye-level it tempts the traveller to a Stendhalian vagary of intention. From this point onwards the catalogue of marvels is too long to compute here; but I must be allowed a passing tribute to the rivers of France, as various as the civilization which has settled along their banks. Golden Loire, barge-loud Seine and puddly Eure, how great is your gift to humanity! Forswearing dalliance, however, we pick our way through the goats which now graze among the ruins of Flaubert's Rouen; allowing the Goujon reliefs at Anet to linger wraith-like before our eyes, and the donjon at Châteaudun to suggest to us an absolute idea of Girth, we head for Switzerland; and only as we pause before the Delacroix in the church at Nantua does it occur to us that our course has been culpably unsteady.

The last few miles of France do their best to provoke the idea of Switzerland, with wooded gorges and sudden vistas of valley towns athwart a fast-running stream; and in courtesy the first miles of Switzerland attempt an equally insufficient idea of France. But the long line of the Jura has not the resonant, winning monotony of the wooded slopes of France; and not until Lac Léman is glimpsed do we sense, in this clear, snow-washed air, the authentic empire of the Swiss idea.

The attraction of the Lake of Geneva is perhaps more readily felt than explained. How otherwise could one take so kindly to this great sulky pan of water, this kidney-bean laid upon the map of Europe? Other lakes have more delicate attractions and a more evenly tolerable climate. Anneçy is more civilized; others besides Wordsworth have been bemused by the "orange gale that o'er Lugano blows"; and for those who see landscape in terms of the theatre, there are the perpendicular excitements of the Walensee. The Lake of Thun is more private; and the lakes of the Campagna still recollect the cheesy gold of Richard Wilson's pigment. Nobody has ever gone very closely into those diffuse and contestable assertions by which, between 1760 and 1820, the name of Lac Léman was hoisted above the reach of reasoned comment. Rousseau himself is now more studied in the lecture-room than in the heart; and although Byron and Shelley

have still the warmth of minor suns, I doubt if many a visitor to
Clarens (15) now tilts his burning-glass in their direction, or catches
fire from the suggestion that in this midge-ridden resort even the
trees

> *. . . take root in love; the snows above,*
> *The very glaciers have his colours caught,*
> *And the sunset into rose-hues sees them wrought*
> *By rays which sleep there lovingly.*

Of course this lingering pink is, as it happens, a permanent and
much-prized feature of Veveyan sunsets; but its amorous connota-
tion is no longer insisted upon, and Byron himself, five years after
his visit, seems to have considered it no more than a rhetorical courtesy. When, indeed, an acquaintance called upon him at the Palazzo
Lanfranchi in Pisa, where he was coasting along upon a diet of claret
and soda-water, he went so far as to say that one visit to Switzerland
was enough for a lifetime. "I never led so moral a life", he complained, "as during my residence in that country; but I gained no
credit by it. On the contrary, there is no story so absurd that they did
not invent at my cost. I was watched by glasses on the other side of
the lake . . . I was waylaid in my evening drives . . . I was accused
of corrupting all the grisettes in the Rue Basse"; in short . . . "they
looked upon me as a man-monster, worse than the *piqueur*." Be that
as it may, poetic signals of discovery went up all through the nineteenth century; and when it was Matthew Arnold's turn to extol

> *That much-loved inland sea,*
> *The ripples of whose blue waves* **cheer**
> *Vevey and Meillerie—*

the elegist of Cumnor and Bablockhythe was able to evoke some of
the facts of landscape which, from 1790 onwards, had been smothered
beneath the great blanket-ideas of Liberty and Revolution. An early
poem, for instance, fills out the picture of an Alpine track with the
information that

> *Behind are the abandoned baths,*
> *Mute in their meadows lone;*

and in middle life Arnold reverted with minute devotion to the
specific pleasures of a walk below Glion—the husks, fresh-heaped and
burning, beneath the chestnut-trees, the new-cut grasses and the

meadows blue with *Gentiana Lutea*. All the same, poets are fickle and spasmodic guides, and I at least would give all Coleridge's passionate vocatives, and his allusions to "thy bald awful head, O sovran Blanc", for a good prose narrative, well dug and dredged.

Such a one exists, moreover. Vine-bordered, moody and large, Lac Léman has been anatomized once and for all by Professor F. A. Forel. Her least variations of temper and appearance found in him, for more than fifty years, a registrar at once genial and exact. All travellers carry within themselves an obstreperous committee of specialist observers; unnoticed at home, these become vocal at the first sight of new ground. Lac Léman calls out the full resources of this inward cabal; but the hydrologer, the chemist, the fisherman, the naval historian, the seismographer and the glutton will find that M. Forel has forestalled their questions; and if they wish to consult this pantomath, they have only to descend to the lower galleries of the London Library and there, squatting on the iron grille, to dust, cut and read his three volumes. Among writers on Switzerland, M. Forel has a place of his own. Where so many are visiting amateurs, he bears the mark of the native professional. Hugo and Lamartine can hoarsen themselves, after the fashion of their age, and sedentary persons may marvel at the medicinal exertions of Sir Leslie Stephen, or of Mr. Smythe and Mr. Lunn. The discreet passion of M. Forel finds a different outlet. In London, his pages give sometimes the effect of an almost English reserve; only, indeed, in the presence of the lake itself can one seize the full gravity and independence of his art; only in the face of its over-demonstrative scenery can we measure his zeal. Nature herself exaggerates in this quarter; only Man—or more exactly, only M. Forel—is above suspicion. When he remarks, of this grandiose and mercurial pond, that it has a volume of 88,920 million cubic metres, a maximum depth of some 950 feet, and an area of 582 square kilometres, the figures have the air of an abstraction; but they have their place in his grand design. All travellers can profit by his work; and when one looks at the *Pêche Miraculeuse* in which, more than five centuries ago, Konrad Witz adapted the New Testament to the landscape of Lac Léman, one can hardly credit that M. Forel was not at hand in 1444 to advise upon the authentic speed of the currents off Thonon.

The lake is best encountered at one of its extremities. One may choose to debouch at Villeneuve, where the delta of the Rhône widens among water-green marshes loud with frogs. To the east, the gaunt secrecies of the Valais stretch on towards Sion and Martigny; here an unsmiling peasantry wears the goitre like a national badge, and as for the theory put forward by Senancour ("*Rien n'est si rare dans la plus grande partie de la Suisse qu'un beau sein . . . beaucoup de femmes du pays n'en ont pas même l'idée"*), there would be small reason to question it here. From the delta itself a primitive pier-head leads out towards open water. Wild flowers sweeten its cobbles, and around the dead body of a swan flies converse in the undertone of connoisseurs. The general prospect is undeniably grand, and may be enhanced by timely sampling of the wine of the neighbourhood. The intake of the Rhône affords M. Forel one of his best-elaborated themes. Roman historians had inferred from the great pace of the Rhône, and the relative heaviness of its waters, that the parent river passed through the lake without mingling its stream with the general mass. Strabo even gave ignorance an Ovidian embellishment by comparing the scene to the fountains of Arethusa, and the fast-flowing Rhône to the magical Alpheus, which retained its freshness even after a passage beneath the sea. Disrespect for the credulities of Marcellinus, Pomponius Mela and the elder Pliny disputed, in the mind of M. Forel, with loyalty to the special qualities of the lake. With the aid of his patent water-spectacles he gazed fixedly at the point where the heavy and opaque water of the reinforcing river first loses its momentum; and with the eye of a Courbet he watched how the darker stream "breaks up into large greasy bobbles or oval clouds, which form a kind of moving staircase as they slowly sink down through the clear water of the lake".

If, again, one first sees the lake from the quays of Geneva, a very different spectacle obtains. In summer the many sluices in the harbour give to each bridge a cooling beard of green and silver; no pavements are hotter than those of Geneva, but all walks through the town must take at length a downward turn, and at last one hears, perhaps at a hundred paces, the assuaging susurrus of the Rhône. Listen for a moment to the comparable jet of Ruskin's eloquence. "Fifteen feet thick, of not flowing, but flying water; not water, neither—melted glacier, one should call it; the force of the ice is with it, and the wreathing of the clouds, the gladness of the sky, and the continuance of Time. . . . Here was one mighty wave that was always itself, and every fluted swirl of it, constant as the wreathing of a shell . . . alike through bright day and lulling night, the never-pausing plunge, and never-fading flash, and never-hushing whisper, and, while the sun was up, the ever-answering glow of unearthly aquamarine, ultramarine, violet-blue, gentian-blue, peacock-blue, river-of-paradise blue. . . ."

Geneva has changed since Ruskin's day, and though one can still drive over the ledges of the Salève, aglow with primrose and soldanelle, the furniture of the lake itself has much altered. The "raft-like flat feluccas" and the "filiform suspension bridge" are gone; and in their stead the traveller crosses upon solid granite, and later, pacing the Edwardian frontage of the north bank, finds himself beneath the sharp beaks of the tethered lake-steamers. The line of these suggests an arrowy swiftness very different from the stealth and labour with which, once a week during the season, they convey their moist Sunday freight of strangers on holiday. But these boats are new-comers, and M. Forel takes no account of them. On the other hand, he is warm, decidedly warm, about the ship-money imposed in 1375 by Amedee VI of Savoy, and he tells us that in 1606 Villeneuve stood at only twelve hours' rowing-distance from Geneva. (The great skill of these professional oarsmen survives, I believe, in the amateur crews, based upon Lausanne, which so surprisingly style themselves "Les Merry Boys".) In the eighteenth century the ships of the Bernese Navy, with their armoured sides, lacquered pavilions and huge, new-varnished bear-mascots in the bows, plied their orna-mental way along Lac Léman, and mock-battles took place in Geneva roads. These are vanished sights, and rank with the "fête of Naviga-tion" which, in August 1849, George Eliot was pleased to enjoy. An excess of rowing made her ill afterwards, but she thought the spectacle quite worth it—"the mingling of the silver and the golden rays on the rippled lake, the bright colours of the boats, the music, the splendid fireworks, and the pale moon looking at it all with a sort of grave surprise, made up a scene of perfect enchantment". Four years earlier her contemporary Flaubert had lodged for a day or two on the Promenade St. Antoine, and recorded a less sociable nocturne. Solitary and bearish at that time, he had taken himself and his cigar to the small public garden in which Pradier's Rousseau sits. A wind band had been playing; flute and trombone aroused in him the mirage of success, the "tremors of fame"; he sat on until it grew cold and the audience slipped away, one by one, from the benches.

Flaubert had every reason to visit Rousseau's island. Not only did he feel a normal piety towards the hero of the scene, but the sculptor also was among his best friends. Pradier had been born in Geneva; and although his mode of life was remote from the sobriety and chastity of Genevese manners, his work was duly honoured in the city. (It may be seen also in the monument on the bastions to the botanist Pyramus de Candolle, and in the La Harpe monument at Rolle.) Pradier and Flaubert were joined together by a quite sym-bolic bond of sympathy and admiration. It was Pradier who advised Flaubert to secure for himself "un amour normal, régulier, nourri et solide"; and it was in Pradier's studio, in a forest of marble and plaster, that Flaubert first encountered the more than marmoreal

14

frame of Madame Colet. Later, when he had yielded to the exasperation of her charms, he paid Pradier the tribute which any artist would be proud to deserve: "he is an excellent man and a great artist; yes, a great artist, a true Greek, and the most ancient of all the moderns; a man who lets nothing distract him—neither politics, nor Fourier, nor the Jesuits, nor the University; and a man who, like a good workman, with his sleeves above the elbow, is there, doing his job from morning till night, in love with his art and longing to do well. Everything is in that: the love of one's art."

The Rousseau monument is one of Pradier's happiest conceptions. Barefooted, and with his nightshirt disposed in Roman folds, the great irritant is discovered with pencil and tablet at the ready. The statue faces the prow of the island, which in its turn is pointing towards the harbour entrance and the open water of the lake. Ourselves must turn, however, and walk through the poplars, past the children with their toffee-apples and the swans regnant on their circular beach, back on to the Pont des Bergues; and there we must consider the central problem of Geneva.

Great cities, like great families, have a rich private history; but these permutations are often hidden beneath the glassy correctitude of the present. Habitual perusers of the Complete Peerage are enabled, however, to put a new value upon the ordinary commerce of civility; their studies equip them with a stereoscope, much as the historian of art can penetrate the defence of varnish, glaze and dirt. With some families it is possible to name the year in which they made a tremendous effort of self-development, put forth a great general, a beauty or an eminent divine, and ever afterwards sank backward into atrophy; in others a streak of maniacal ambition is constant, or some regular, predictable form of disaster in personal relations. In some, the house of Reputation is annually put in order; in others, a parrot raves in those deserted saloons and the front door droops from the jamb. With cities it is much the same. At Troy, little remains but a ring of earthworks, a many-winded plain and the pride of a great name; in more recent casualties, in Rouen or Vienna, the grandeurs of the past exert a crippling fascination upon those condemned to live on in the present. In others, more fortunate, a traditional mode of life has been resumed, but under how great a load of self-imputed guilt! In most cities one is aware not of the past in general but of a moment in the past. At Dijon or Avignon, for instance, there can be no doubt of the point at which the present must feel the tug of the past. Geneva, on the other hand, is one of the few great cities of Europe in which nearly every period has been interesting. More: it is one of the great cities of the present. One of

15

the last museums of solid middle-class living, it has the instantaneous attraction of a large and beautiful city in perfect physical health. The traditional severity of Genevese life may still be the rule in the closed society of the city; and the equally traditional mastery of commerce and the law may, indeed must obviously, still nourish and implement the general scene; but wealth and security have given Geneva a bloom of gaiety and good living which is peculiarly attractive to foreign visitors. In no way a frivolous city, Geneva is none the less an excellent, most pliable centre for frivolity. Exquisite as may have been, under Calvin, its perception of good and evil, and memorable, under Voltaire, the forbidden pleasures of the private theatre, and merciful, in nearly every age, the possibility of asylum within its boundaries, yet Geneva can never have been more agreeable than it is to-day. It is an expensive city, and those who see Switzerland as a land of plenty would be surprised to find how many of its inhabitants go hungry; but in general Geneva is fortunately placed. Only eighty years ago it could be said (and by a panegyrist of the city) that "Geneva is a little England, an industrial society in which extremes of misery and opulence are in dangerous proximity to each other. Filthy streets, the breeding-pens of sickness and indigence, run up to the foot of the lofty quarter of the old aristocracy. The Genevese workman knows nothing of comfort or security; his salary, his very livelihood, are daily endangered; the disgusting hovels in which he works and sleeps are scorching in summer and ice-cold in winter: small wonder if he consoles himself with drink". "In 1830," according to the same authority, "the lower town was as it had been in the Middle Ages. The main street, the Rues Basses, where once fairs were held, was blocked by the *dômes* (projecting roofs supported on pillars of wood) and by two rows of wooden stalls. The quarter by the lake and along the Rhône was hideous to look upon. Dilapidated ramparts, old chains hanging from rotting wooden piles, timber-yards, slaughter-houses and filthy hutments, half of wood and half of stone, slowly collapsing into the water. When steamboats began to bring tourists within sight of these abominations, the authorities decided to rebuild that part of Geneva."

Tourists are often insensitive to such sights, and Théophile Gautier was no exception. He was delighted by the *dômes*, and compared them to a routed army of cavalry, with their horses spinning head over heels; also to "those acrobats whom the English call acropedestrians, and who, lying on their backs with their feet in the air, send a log of wood or a couple of children flying high above them". The riverside hutments pleased him even better. Architecturally of the lowest, most ramshackle complexion, they were "worm-eaten, blackened, split, cracked, green with decay, bleary and seasoned, and altogether as leprous and calloused as Bonington and Decamps could wish; the windows were full of holes half-closed with broken glass; and from them hung the garlands of tripe and offal of pork which served, in these agreeable lodgings, for floral decoration". Opposite were tanneries, where whole skins were hung from beams and left to soak in the river. To all this has succeeded the urbane and stately waterfront of to-day: the hotel patronized by Henry James, the cafés papered with the grinning nonentities of 1929, the Jardin Anglais so carefully tended, the miraculous displays of tobacco and watches, the kiosks a-flower with the magazines of every country in the world, the elegant, accessible ladies of the pavement, and in the evening a nocturne beyond the appetite of Whistler. All this part of Geneva, and the double row of shopping streets behind, is a nineteenth- and twentieth-century creation. It provides that impulse of activity without which an old town will quietly petrify in the summer and in the winter go as quietly damp and sour. But one need walk only a few yards to find the other Geneva. Even at waterside level there is, for example, the Temple Neuf in the Place de la Fusterie. This was built between 1707 and 1710 by Vennes, whose mark may be seen also in the Hôtel de Ville and on the Bourg-de-Four; careful restoration has not destroyed the character of this baroque edifice, and its pillared, octagonal interior may still be admired; the design, for all its discretion of style, refutes Gautier's contention that in Geneva "the curve and the ellipse are forbidden, being too sensual, too voluptuous". The neighbouring Place du Molard has changed considerably since Bonington's time, but it has retained the appearance of a square in some small market-town. There are many cafés, an excellent print-shop and a profusion of flowers. Here, and in the adjoining alleys, Geneva comes nearest to France. Here are conceived some of Switzerland's most generous tributes to French art and literature: the definitive editions of Bergson and Malraux, the periodical *Labyrinthe* and many a sumptuous homage to the École de Paris. These few acres are important to Switzerland and important to Europe: for here dead art and dead literature have no place. In the cafés round the Molard the ritual of excited comment about Genêt and Henry Miller is carried on within the more sober scheme of traditional Genevese life; and in the same tiny room, with its long mirror, fivefold row of bottles and central corkscrew staircase of iron, impenetrable ancients will sit in silence while the juvenile savants of the quarter, each enlaced with his bare-legged inspiratrix, composedly savage the contributors to *Horizon* and *Les Temps Modernes*.

"Does the road wind uphill all the way?" The plaintive accents of Christina Rossetti must accompany visitors to many a Swiss town, and this not least in Geneva. Only mount, however, through some convenient gap in this great twentieth-century bazaar, and you will presently encounter the Geneva of the Cathedral, the Bourg-de-Four, the Hôtel de Ville and the Promenade de la Treille. Contrary to common belief, this part of Geneva is not at all Gothic in tone; nor is it especially Calvinist. Drastic and permanent as was the effect of the Reformation upon Genevese life, it left the city itself relatively unchanged. An English visitor, always mindful of the fantastic opulence of our monumental tradition, may feel that a cathedral without fine tombs is hardly a cathedral at all; but once in the open again he will applaud the simple grandeur of the old town, and the art, unknown to modern England, with which municipal buildings of capital splendour have been made to blend with their neighbours.

The Reform did not make its way unchallenged in Geneva. The city has traditions older than that of Protestantism, and when it was proposed that vigilant elders should watch and report upon the habits of their fellow-citizens, there were many ("irreverent and emancipated men," according to one historian, "firm of heart and ready of arm") who asserted an earlier allegiance. This was the first rebuff to Calvin; he had been passing through Geneva in 1536 when Guillaume Farel, a Reformer of long standing and more than thirty years his senior, pressed him repeatedly to stay. The "awful adjurations" (Calvin's own phrase) of the older militant rarely failed of their effect. Calvin doubted if the time was yet ripe; "things had not yet assumed the right shape", he said afterwards; but he stayed.

Irreligion, at that time, disturbed the Reformers even more than the religion of Rome; and when a temporary reaction drove Farel to Neuchâtel and Calvin to Strasbourg, the city was given over to the ingenious debauches of the young. After they had spent a certain time in gambling, whoring and dancing naked through the streets to the sound of fife and tambourine, the natural tenor of Genevese life reasserted itself and the Reformers hurried back—eager, one must presume, to lay redoubled stripes upon the back of the repining city. Castigation was more natural to Farel than to his young and sensitive colleague. Calvin at that time resembled rather a junior member of the Oxford Movement than that legendary thurifer, the man of fire and ice. A peaceable stripling, of literary tastes (the author, one must remember, of a commentary upon Seneca's *Clementia*), he was frankly relieved when things got out of hand at Geneva and he was able to retire to Strasbourg, and there cultivate his conscience in peace. "By nature timid, soft and pusillanimous," he wrote of himself,

"I was more pleased, when they turned me out, than I ought to have been. And being thenceforth at liberty, and absolved from my charge, I intended to live a quiet life, and never again to take up any public duties." And when, in 1540, the Reformers urged him to return to Geneva, he replied that, "Whenever I recall the miserable hours which I spent at Geneva, I cannot but tremble from top to toe at the idea of going back there. Why should I plunge again into that devouring gulf?"

He went back, none the less; and he remained in Geneva until he died, in 1564. Some of his great qualities were foreseeable. The graduate of Paris, Orleans and Bourges was more than a match for the disputants of Geneva. In personal relations Calvin could show, when he pleased, a most exquisite and attaching sensibility. He was at his ease in all classes of society, and he attended with melodious despatch to a body of correspondence which, by its volume alone, would have taxed a more ordinary frame. In his handling of his small but mettlesome flock he was influenced by an historical model; finding that in the first three centuries of the Christian era the un-worthy were forbidden to go to Communion, he decided to accord this privilege only to those who had proved themselves worthy. Not only did this invest his rule with the dignity of an heroic episode in human history, but it ennobled that most permanent of human traits: the instinct to interfere in other people's business. Prompted in his own case by a laudable spirit of vigilance and self-criticism, this system of mutual scrutiny became in the end an organized traffic in spying and delation. At its worst, it produced such infamies as the burning of Servetus. Let the greatest of English historians speak for this. "I am more deeply scandalized at the single execution of Servetus," writes Gibbon, "than at the hecatombs which have blazed in the Auto da Fés of Spain and Portugal. (1) The zeal of Calvin seems to have been envenomed by personal malice, and per-haps envy. He accused his adversary before their common enemies, the Judges of Vienna, and betrayed, for his destruction, the sacred trust of a private correspondence. (2) The deed of cruelty was not varnished by the pretence of danger to the church or state. In his passage through Geneva, Servetus was a harmless stranger, who neither preached, nor printed, nor made proselytes. A Catholic in-quisitor yields the same obedience which he requires, but Calvin violated the golden rule of doing as he would be done by; a rule which I read in a moral treatise of Isocrates, four hundred years be-fore the publication of the Gospel." It has been argued, from the other side, that the trial and condemnation of Servetus were the work of lay magistrates over whom Calvin had no control, and to whom, indeed, he had on occasion to apologize. One cannot, however, forget so easily that Calvin later persecuted, and did his best to ruin, the ablest of his critics on that occasion, his former colleague Sebastian Castalion. The hesitant Calvin of 1538 had become, by 1553, an energumen to whom all opposition, however honourable, was a thing to be scotched. It is more profitable to reflect upon other features of his work. Himself an intellectual, he founded in 1559 the Académie de Genève; before long there were twenty printing-shops in Geneva, and the city became, as it has remained, a fortress of the Protestant mind. All were welcomed who chose, for reasons of conscience, to make Geneva their home; by 1564 there had arrived the fifteen hundred French families, the three hundred Italian families, and the smaller companies of Spaniards, English and Flemings who were to make of Geneva a little Europe. (After St. Bartholomew's Eve, in 1572, more than two thousand French families were given asylum at Geneva.)

The society which resulted had many excellent and remarkable sides; above all, it presented so solid, so united a rampart against its enemies that, even forty years after Calvin's death, the city could repel a well-mounted surprise attack. Calvin himself had devised a form of religion which was at once attractive to the simplest intelligence and susceptible of genuine intellectual elucidation. The natural moderation of the Swiss temperament ensured that the severity of Calvinism did not lead, as it has led elsewhere, to pathological deformities of character; and the Genevese were empowered, by the habit of self-denial, to survive the disagreeable periods of want and disease which recurred throughout Calvin's ministry. Upon the faces of these grave monitors were united, it would seem, the pallor of the student and the chagrin of the exile; Ronsard and du Bellay describe, and perhaps heighten, the sickly, remorseful ill-temper of the less contented reformers; and certainly there is a humourless gravity in the ordinances of 1560, with their proscription of velvet, embroidery, silk stockings, waved or false hair, large wedding-parties and pendants of silver or gold. Yet Geneva has never been the home of extremes; when it was found necessary to expel a society of nuns from the city, they were escorted to the borders of the Arve by a select company of elders, each of whom gave an arm to one of the ladies; and now that it has reverted to a less stringent mode of life, one may trace with equanimity the sources of its power.

Elsewhere in Switzerland, the Town Hall is a building of hieratic majesty, singled out by paintings, extensive and carefully restored, upon the exterior walls, or (as at Neuchâtel) by the impact of foreign elegance upon the indigenous, provincial style of the adjacent square.

At Geneva there is none of this: not even a break in the conventional face of the narrow street. The "grey old high-featured house-masks", of which Henry James took note, are displaced by no vulgar municipal pomp. The sober, unyielding façades of the rue de l'Hôtel de Ville do none the less represent, for the first time in the architectural history of the city, a certain triumph of amenity. The medieval house-fronts of Geneva were generally narrow and uncomely. Land was divided up into lengthy wafers, stretching at right angles to the street; and where space allowed, the front of the house was often obscured by a *dôme* or projecting gallery. Only after the failure of the Savoyard Escalade in 1605 did the senior citizens begin to build in a less primitive style; and in 1617 were begun the present façade of the Hôtel de Ville and the neighbouring Maison Turettini. Both were built by Jean Pattac after the plans of Faule Petitot, and they constitute a recognizable nucleus of belated Renaissance building. The Turettini palace is in itself an epitome of Genevese social history. François Turettini was a silk-merchant, born in Lucca, who came to Geneva in 1592, after spending eighteen years as a Protestant exile from Italy. In twenty-five years he became one of the wealthiest men in the city, and his town house has an amplitude and a sense of display which are quite new in Geneva. A few years later Turettini's son-in-law, Vincent Burlamaqui, built (rue de la Cité 8) a large house in a cognate style; and a persistent visitor will be able to identify other examples of seventeenth-century façades in the Maison Micheli, rue de l'Hôtel de Ville 5, the Maison Calandrini, Grand-Rue 39, and (appreciably later) the Maison Rigot, 20 rue de la Cité. Yet it is still from the Hôtel de Ville that we can draw most pleasure; Pattac and Petitot garnished their façade with two portals of the utmost grandeur, and within (dating from 1556) is the four-sided, stairless ramp devised by Jean and Nicolas Bogueret during Calvin's régime; to them also do we owe the inner doorway, which, with its proud inscription "Post Tenebras Lux 1566", is in its more delicate way the counterpart of its English contemporary, the Gate of Virtue at Caius College, Cambridge. The extreme sobriety of all the other architectural forms of the period gives to these gateways a most welcome bloom of poetry.

This quarter can show many other relics of the sixteenth and seventeenth centuries: the arcaded Arsenal, for instance, which even in d'Alembert's time was stocked in earnest. But we can no longer defer examination of the Cathedral. (Cathedral it may be called, though local custom names it the Temple de St. Pierre.) This is an endearing rather than a beautiful building, and is perhaps best seen from the east, with the episcopal stables at its foot. The west end was entirely done over, between 1752 and 1756, and fitted with a monumental portico in classical style, supported by six Corinthian columns. Influenced, it would appear, by the Pantheon of Agrippa, and designed by Benedetto Alfieri, a near relation of the poet, this portico has never failed to irritate those for whom the Gothic is sacred and the classical profane. Let great Burckhardt speak for the other side: "In itself of great beauty," he wrote, "it is so exceptionally high that when standing in front of it one can see only very little of the rest of the building. Nor need one regret the former façade, because it is apparent from old prints that it was quite out of harmony with the rest of the building." Burckhardt was only nineteen when he wrote this passage, but his words may prompt some visitors to look with less prejudice upon the west end of the Cathedral.

The interior of the Cathedral has been very thoroughly restored; and one must go to the Musée d'Art et d'Histoire if one wishes to see a part of what must have been its finest embellishment—the reredos executed in 1444 by Conrad Witz. The use of a field-glass will reveal, however, some uncommonly good capitals. Few visitors, of course, are moved by exclusively æsthetic considerations; and if one feels a certain awe when entering St. Pierre, or the little chapel beside it, in which Calvin and John Knox once preached, it is less from pleasure in the rather indifferent forms which confront one than from the confused, composite genius of the place itself. The upper part of Geneva is like the fourth storey of a house in some ancient market square. The ground-floor may have been cut away and turned into offices, but up above the old façade is intact, and behind it the dear lumber of many generations—the medals from Fontenoy and Inkerman, the engravings after Lely and Wouvermans, the seatless wicker chairs and the square trunks filled with miscellaneous and perhaps disquieting trophies. (The former Maison Micheli, rue de l'Hôtel de Ville 5, fulfils exactly the Swiss equivalent of this image.) Thus it is that, in the severe precincts of St. Pierre, some may recall that Apollo is said to have been worshipped upon this very site; as Mr. Elliot Felkin has remarked, "His image survived, under the semblance of the sun, in the medieval arms of the city, until in 1418 Pope Martin V substituted the initials of our Lord, as being more suitable." Be this as it may, the great old lumber-room up on the hill above the Léman is not easily to be exhausted. As we pause in the Bourg-de-Four to buy ducks' eggs and Johannisberg Mont d'Or, or search for one of the monographs of local history which the Librairie Jullien has published for more than a century, it is worth remembering that this same square was almost certainly

15   The Ile de Clarens near Montreux

16   Voltaire's Château at **Ferney.**   *From a contemporary print*

17   Geneva : the Place Neuve and Musée Rath,
     with the Mur de la Treille behind

18   Geneva : the arcaded entrance to the Hôtel de Ville

a *forum* in Roman times, and the preferred resort of the retired official. Under Calvin, Geneva became something very rare—the citadel of an idea; but, as Ramuz remarked, ideas are an impermanent basis for a great city. "Protestantism", he said, "had become nothing but a habit, and it ended by being nothing but a name." Fortunately, the old town of Geneva has other resources, and its architecture has profited by them.

The big houses of the seventeenth century were mostly private constructions. Often they served to remind some prosperous family of its Italian origins; but in every case they were sober buildings, and the display-piece, or *Prunkbau*, was unknown. In the eighteenth century, by contrast, the city itself began to plan ensembles of fine town-houses in the French style; and in this way were sponsored two at least of the most spectacular *massifs* of Geneva—those in the rue des Granges and the rue Beauregard. In 1705 a private individual, J. A. Lullin, bought up the ground on which was built, between 1707 and 1712, the present Maison de Saussure. This stands on high ground above the Corraterie, whose mean-faced façade dates from more than a century later; and in the confrontation one can savour the brief triumph of wealth and arrogance, and the revenge, so lasting and so summary, of the commercial, democratic genius of the city. The offices of the Corraterie enshrine an almost American frenzy of business activity; shirt-sleeved executives pace the Turkey carpet, suppliants cower in an adjacent room and, pad in hand, the stenographer sits passive as an antique Prudence. Through the windows (closed and bolted in torrid July) is glimpsed the garden front of Abeille's masterpiece. Is there discernible upon its towering mask a lingering disdain? We cannot tell, for conscientious restoration has robbed it of the embellishments of age and decay. A hundred yards farther, in the Place Neuve, we are faced with the asymmetrical splendours of a later Geneva (17). Elsewhere a city of crevices, Geneva here assumes new grandeurs of space and perspective. To the north, the admirable houses (1720–3) of the rue des Granges; to the north-east, the Promenade de la Treille, a bastion swathed and fronded with creepers, with the Reformation monument at its foot. To the east, the Palais Eynard, an all too faithful piece of Hellenic enthusiasm; amateurs of the Greek Revival will prefer the Musée Rath, built in 1826, at the other end of the square.

Plunge into the wooded centre of this great open space, and you will find, as if in some Platonic grove, the University buildings; these were designed in the sixties of the last century by the architect of the Grand Hotel Palace at Vevey. At a distance is that least Genevese of buildings, the Municipal Theatre. A diminutive version of the Paris

Opera, it accords ill with the restrained grandeurs of its site. Nor has it ever quite established itself as a part of the city. No resident company inhabits it, and when for once, some thirty years ago, Geneva harboured a theatrical venture of the first importance, the company in question had almost to beg its way into the Maison Communale in the Plainpalais. The Pitoeffs were luckier in their audience than in their theatre; one memoir has described how "one could see there, elbow to elbow, though unknown to one another, Lenin, Stravinsky, Lugné-Poe, Einstein, Ramuz. . . ." Strindberg, Tchehov, Maeterlinck, Goldoni and Synge enraptured a part, and a part only, of the Genevese public. Is there, perhaps, in the others some inherited resistance to the pleasures of the theatre? It is certain, in any case, that they have never quite yielded to the blandishments of d'Alembert, who promised them that the theatre "would form the taste of the citizen, and give him those nuances of tact, and that delicacy in sentiment, which it is otherwise very difficult to acquire; literature would profit by it, and libertinage not be increased; Geneva would unite the cultivation of Athens with the discipline of Sparta". No audiences, however, are more grudging than those of Geneva, where the masterworks of Racine, Shakespeare and the aged Verdi are sat out with a more-than-English impassivity.

A great deal more could be said of the physical aspect of Geneva—the spacious avenues (a sort of grandiloquent Cheltenham) near the Musée d'Art et d'Histoire; Carouge, a township of the eighteenth century; the straight-backed houses along the Arve, pearly with *molasse*; the solitary, well-loved plume of water which spouts above the bathing-beach; the little shops off the rue du Mont Blanc, where the gaze of the *flâneur* is suddenly returned by a Milanese pigeon or a marmoset; the ponderous flattery of the big hotels along the Quai du Mont Blanc, and the more acceptable attentions of those on the opposite bank, in which the kings of the currant-market debate in Arabic upon Empire canapés; the travelling circus in the Plainpalais, near which the dry, thin air of the city is suddenly fragrant with the princely and aromatic droppings of an elephant; the bookshop in the Grand' Rue, whose owner, as indifferent to commerce as the antiquaires of Pekin, croons for ever over his Elzevirs; and the great waterside parks, each one a turfy Eden. Our own generation has not contributed much to the scene; a block of flats by Le Corbusier in the rue St. Laurent and his Maison de Verre in the rue Adrien Lachenal have not affected its general character. The League of Nations Building is certainly imposing, though the ideas which it imposes are not perhaps those which its designers would have wished. (Amateurs of painting should inspect the four big decorations

by Bonnard, Vuillard, K. X. Roussel and Maurice Denis; for
these, though strikingly unsuccessful, are one of the curiosities of
twentieth-century painting.)

If, in general, Geneva has retained the good features of every age
in its history, and as successfully sloughed all the bad, it has not been
achieved by mere passive good taste. The unsmiling elevations of
Calvin's city were preserved by vigilance and energy; and if Geneva
is still ennobled by the Francophile palaces of a later age, these have
not been secured without effort. Twice, in 1734 and in 1846, the
citizens of Geneva rose and defeated the oligarchical party. "You
have no conception", wrote Dickens in 1846, "of the preposterous,
insolent little aristocracy of Geneva: the most ridiculous caricature
the fancy can suggest of what we know in England." When other
pleasures are proscribed, those of the intellect unexpectedly flourish;
for this reason the people of Geneva were well able in the early
eighteenth century to resist the allure of French domination; and
when, in December 1813, Geneva slipped free of the Napoleonic
yoke, a nucleus of fine men was at hand to generate afresh the sense
of civic pride. I have not space to disentangle the stages by which
Geneva, like Switzerland itself, has painfully achieved its present
equilibrium. Nor shall I insult my readers by presuming to remind
them of the influence of Rousseau upon his native city. English
visitors may reflect with pleasure, however, upon our several kindly
links with Geneva—among them the relations between Newton and
J. A. Turettini, the influence of the Bibliothèque Britannique in the
early nineteenth century, and the years in which Francis Danby,
exiled from Victorian England, found in Geneva unlimited credit
and, in the end, enthusiastic buyers for his paintings. So numerous
are those who have brought lustre to the name of Geneva that it is
difficult to conclude upon any one representative note. The city, as
Sainte-Beuve remarked, is in size "a dwarf pear-tree, but one which
bears enough fruit for a whole orchard". The great critic went on to
say that Calvin was "its saint, and Abauzit its sage". It would be a
pleasure to think that Abauzit is really the secular patron of the city,
and that behind the wealth and show of Geneva there lingers the
outlook of this legendary, this almost oriental savant. Great learning
does not often bring happiness or generosity of mind, but for
Abauzit, who died in 1767 at the age of eighty-eight, it was a
source of disinterested amenity. Let the irascible pundits of our own
time reflect upon Bonstetten's account of Abauzit in his old age:
"His contentment in poverty, and the serenity of his mind, always
filled me with admiration. If he were alone in his house, and had no
oil for his lamp, he would sing away in his armchair, as happy as a

child. . . . He had an income of thirty louis, which is not much in Geneva; but with it, he lived happier than any king, venerated, almost adored, by everyone around him." Would such virtue still be rewarded in Geneva? Let us conspire to think so, and to rebut the insinuation of Stendhal that "if you see anyone jump out of a window in Geneva, do not hesitate to follow his example: there's sure to be ten per cent. in it".

Most visitors to Switzerland make their way out of Geneva along the lake-road to Nyon and Lausanne. Geography has made it difficult for them to do otherwise, in that the canton of Geneva is islanded in French territory. Before leaving, however, one should not fail to explore the Savoyard shore of the lake. Hermance, the frontier-town, is the natural limit of such a promenade, but the connoisseur of summer-resorts should press on into France as far as Evian. On the way he will pass through wooded farmlands; the northern, more usual shore will seem merely the featureless boundary of the lake, and Geneva itself may become softened, almost vaporized in the heat of the afternoon. Such is the weather in which to visit the Villa Diodati at Cologny. On a clear day it is all too apparent that, since Byron's time, the lake-verges have been ruined, and the celestial prospect toned down to something hardly superior to the Welsh Harp at Hendon. Dull weather sets, moreover, the authentic atmosphere of Byron's stay. "Really," he wrote to Samuel Rogers, "we have had lately such stupid mist, fogs and perpetual density, that one would think Castlereagh had the Foreign Affairs of the Kingdom of Heaven also on his hands." The Villa itself has enough ground to be still a most delectable property. A square building of three storeys, it is arcaded on the ground-floor; above these, an elegant balcony of wrought iron encircles the main rooms of the house. These are Louis XVI saloons of very passable splendour; only in the crucial eighteen inches below the ceiling, and in a certain dullness of ornament, do they fall below standard. Prints of the period often show Byron at work on the balcony; but in general he had felt ill and unsociable throughout his stay. Unable to speak French and repelled by the tone of Genevese society, he saw mostly such old friends or acquaintances as Shelley, Monk Lewis and Hobhouse. Shelley later took a house nearby, at Montalègre, and this may also be seen, though with less pleasure. For the rest, the Château El-Masr, built between 1865 and 1881 in the "English neo-Gothic style" for an English enthusiast, should be remarked; and Professor H. W. Häusermann's researches have lately revealed that the house occupied by Shelley at Montalègre was later the house of Francis Danby, A.R.A., during his years in Geneva.

26

The road to Hermance reveals several excellent small manor-houses. The landscape becomes sensibly more French, until at Hermance itself the Swiss elements of neatness and good repair are pleasantly absent. The crumbling jetty and unfrequented waterfront of the frontier village are places in which loafing becomes a duty; nor is there, as occurs almost everywhere in Switzerland, the mortifying contrast of other people's activity. Hermance drowses, and ourselves drowse with it. Evian, on the other hand, is so singular a town that I must go outside my mandate in order to describe it. After passing through Thonon, Amphion must command our respect, so impregnated is it with the souvenirs of its day of fashion, under the Second Empire; literature, moreover, must be allowed to have followed fashion, since in the garden of the Villa Brancovan there is a plaque which commemorates the estivations, in infancy, of Anna de Noailles.

Evian itself is perhaps two miles farther on. It consists of a dilapidated little harbour, upon which has been clamped the conventional mask of a watering-place. The Quai Baron-de-Blonay suggests one interpretation of Evian; at right angles to it, alleys fragrant with fruit, vegetables and rotting pulp suggest quite another; while in the main street the medicinal aspect is given full play. One may take the waters either in privacy or in elaborate alcoves of Oriental design. So profuse are the springs that at one point they gush out freely from a hole in the wall; and here the delegates of thrift or indigence gather daily with bottle and jug. (The water itself has a flavour so flavourless as to assume the proportions of a philosophical problem.) The shallow box-windows of village shops have been lined with strip-lighting and filled with the jetsam of the Parisian season; but the street in general invites one only to modest expenditures of an invalidish type. Once on the waterfront, another spirit presides. Mr. Pleasure (for such is his democratic style) stirs with a bare foot the golden dust of the boulevard, ruffles the foliage of the arbours to let in the noonday sun, and dictates even the gait, lazy but watchful, of the municipal boatmen. Evian has one great advantage over its more cleanly *vis-à-vis*: everything in its south-lying, sun-welcoming crescent avows, if not abandon itself, at any rate the possibility of abandon. As if in token of this, personable ladies recline offshore in ornamental, upholstered swans—symbolizing, it may be, a predicament which, since the time of Leda, has retained an element of pleasurable confusion.

Evian is a town in which high and low (I speak now in financial terms) enjoy themselves equally; but they do not necessarily enjoy themselves together. On the slopes above Evian there has been erected an hotel of almost comical luxury. It would be tempting to

call this the company director's Shangri-La, did this not imply
some disrespect to an ingenious body of men. A screen of
firs obscures the town below. Between lake and sky (both newly
azured) the wraith of the northern shore hangs at a respectful distance, in readiness for the moment at dusk when it drapes a new
constellation across the darkening sky. Beatitude is here for the ask-
ing. White-coated acolytes pad silently to anticipate one's whims.
When faced with a new pilgrim, only recently unloaded from the
Edwardian coachwork of the hotel's private omnibus, they will
address him, as if by divination, in an elegant version of his own
vernacular. (English visitors may count upon an almost Wildean
grace of diction.) The novice's feet become bogged in the "deep
pile" familiar to novel-readers; large, unsubtle meals help him to
pass the day quickly; and if intellectual yearnings should seize him,
the illustrated papers of four continents lie next his arm. But
Switzerland is our concern, and we must regain it; this can be done
by boat, or by motoring on into the Valais, or by returning to
Geneva. If this last course be adopted, there will be time to visit
another curiosity: the little township of Carouge, where one may still
discern traces of the project formed towards 1780 by King Victor
Amadeus II of Savoy. This monarch had hoped to turn Carouge,
then only a very modest village on the Arve, into a rival of Geneva—
a *Provinzhauptort* exemplary in elegance, and geometrical in plan.
For lack of money, the greater part of this project was abandoned, and
even the royal palace had in 1808 to be put to commercial use. A
town hall, a hospital and some simple residences remain, however,
and the Catholic church, the Sainte-Croix, originated in the same
period. In the 1820s it was done over, and the Protestant church was
designed and built by Louis Bagutti in firmly Hellenistic style.

Eventually one must leave Geneva. Other cities, other climes,
other languages invite our patronage; but an encouraging feature of
our removal is that, for the present, M. Forel is still a good guide.
He is particularly sound on winds, which so largely mould the climate
of Lac Léman. He evokes, with the skill of a novelist, their varying
natures until, for example, the night-walking Morget, the centrifugal,
onshore Rebat and the powerful and deleterious Sudois assume the
familiarity of characters from the *Forsyte Saga* or *Les Hommes de
Bonne Volonté*. In two other cases, these winds attain an almost
Balzacian will and independence. In literature, as in life, the lugu-
brious and insistent Bise du Nord dominates the scene with its cold,
damp and regular breathing. Towards the Rhône delta the Vaudois
offers a more enlivening commentary upon lakeside existence, for
this hot, dry wind, with its sudden and authoritative arrivals and

departures is a great traveller, refreshed and exhilarated by its passage across the Alps. Much of the emotional ambience of Lac Léman should be ascribed to these agents of ecstasy and despair. The extremes of passion, for instance, in Rousseau's *Julie*: does not Saint-Preux speak of the "cold *bise*" which has brought down the ice and snow? "All nature is dying before my eyes," he writes, "and with it dies the hope in my heart." A few miles farther west, this damaging comparison might never have occurred to him. But for the *bise*, Julie and Saint-Preux and Mylord Edouard Bomston could have got out more; stuffing indoors and writing all those letters, they erected a local climatic misfortune into a first principle of the heart. M. Forel is more matter-of-fact.

To the natural historian, Lac Léman has no great appeal. M. Forel loyally names the shrew-mouse, the plover, the stork and the coot among other visitors to the area, but in general it is the odd and the irregular which catches his eye—an interesting case of suicide among frogs, for instance, or the involuntary visits of otters to the harbour area of Geneva. In 1837 swans were introduced to the lake at the whim of a bus-conductor, who brought two of them from Paris. The descendants of this hardy and fecund pair now ornament the whole length of the lake. With the air of a man noting the dates of Ascot or Goodwood, M. Forel remarks that "their caresses may be observed from the 5th to the 20th of March". From time to time he observed and noted in the interests of learning, curious instances of sexual precocity and corruption among these swans; and he may have had hopes of finding a similar deplorable inventiveness among tortoises. But alas! The anti-scientific attitude of certain Venetian merchants rendered such studies quite fruitless; from 1845 onwards they imported so many of these creatures that the aboriginal tortoise, native to the Rhône marshes, could no longer be distinguished. Driven under water by this disappointment, M. Forel researched with more success into the lake's fine complement of fish. The delicious perch, so welcome upon Genevese tables, was the object of particular attention. The sociable young perchettes assume in his narrative the ambivalent allure of *jeunes filles en fleur*; and as for the lonely and philosophical adults, each one a finny Thoreau beside his chosen boulder, they provide a rare point of repose in this agitated area. The bull-head, the ablet and the bleak cannot wrest our affection from the speciality of Lac Léman—the delicate féra. To this most tender of fish, all other waters are mortal; and he can only be best enjoyed when, secure in his buttery overcoat, he is eaten within earshot of the lake. A respectful ear must be cocked to M. Forel's story of the blind shrimp, or *Niphargus Foreli*, which lives in the perpetual darkness of the lowest depths of the lake. The worm peculiar to the area, the *Bythonomus Lémani*, may be left to more specialized tastes; most readers, I feel sure, will take it, its transparent skin and its 40–62 segments, on trust. It is quite otherwise with the creature most summarily treated by M. Forel—Man; our teacher's powers of embrace, elsewhere more reminiscent of the panther or grizzly bear than of the savant, seem here to have failed him. Man's case is even worse than that of the tortoise—so great and so constant has been the admixture of foreign strains. This may, however, be precisely the point of most interest for many of those who are attracted by Lac Léman and happen one day to alight upon its super-serviceable shores.

★   ★   ★   ★   ★

In a letter dated March 1819 and written to his sister Fanny, Keats described the ideal, the paradisial life for a goldfish. Safe in an enormous bowl of ever-changing water, embowered in myrtle and japonica, the fortunate fish was to peer out through a handsome painted window. "I should like the window to open on to the Lake of Geneva," Keats went on, "and then I'd sit and read all day, like the picture of somebody reading." Keats never went to Switzerland, and could not have gauged the distracting power of his chosen landscape. The importunate grandeur of the scene had, in his time, a correlative in human affairs. Over-excited republicans and gasping pantheists found, once and for all, a landscape perfectly accommodated to their state of mind. Love and liberty were decidedly the things that mattered most; and Lamartine, in his *Ressouvenir du Léman*, spoke for every foreign visitor:

> *L'amour, la liberté, ces alcyons du monde,*
> *Combien de fois ont-ils pris leur vol sur ton onde,*
> *Ou confié leur nid à tes flots transparents?*

These large, flat sentiments are now without meaning; and the landscape which inspired them can be at times so potently and intimately tedious that the visitor feels within himself a great heave of boredom and impatience, comparable to the *seiches* or mysterious rhythmic disturbances which agitate the lake itself. At these moments, illustrious blacklegs come to mind: Gérard de Nerval, remarking that at Lausanne even the steeples were awkward and provincial; Voltaire, sticking out a damp winter at Prangins and declaring that, furred, booted and caulked as he was, he was none the less dying of rage and cold. Stendhal, however, could not but make a gesture of admiration as he stood off Vevey in the steam-packet *Aigle*. The great height of the mountains which, with their dark woods, tore down towards the lake at an angle of perhaps sixty degrees, gave to the scene a quality of instantaneous tragedy; but the foreground was dull, he thought, and not comparable to the lakes of Lombardy. Life on the *Aigle* had other defects—gaseous lemonade, a surfeit of Calvinist tracts and the naturally glum and unyielding manners of the Genevois. Even the occupational gaiety of sailors was not proof against this local chill and constraint. The Italian amenities so rightly dear to Stendhal were still rarer on shore, but he tried hard to find subjects for amiable comment. The system of government, for instance, had a likably paternal element in it; and though he could not warm to Calvin or to the variant of English Methodism which seemed to have taken hold in Geneva, he noted that it did at least solve one serious problem— the answer to which, in his view, would decide, one way or another, the nature of twentieth-century civilization. Democracy and an authoritarian religion were incompatible aims; and, between these two, Calvin had effected a working compromise. Like Gibbon, Stendhal was teased and held captive by the closed, autonomous societies in which unmarried girls were allowed to lead lives of their own—"trusted to their own prudence," in Gibbon's phrase, "among a crowd of young men of every nation in Europe". These eminent, hard-working but on the whole strikingly unsuccessful flirts were both transfixed by the delicate possibilities of such a system; but long residence in Switzerland forced Gibbon to concede that "the invisible line between liberty and licentiousness was never transgressed by a gesture, a word, or a look . . . a singular institution, expressive of the innocent simplicity of Swiss manners". But when all this had been said, Geneva was still the city pinned down by Voltaire in a single line:

On y calcule et jamais on n'y rit.

Its people were rich, but with no power of enjoying their wealth; well read, but not enlightened; cheerless and prudent in their recreations; and in the cast of their minds emphatic, reasonable and sad. The delicious fact of sex had for them the remoteness of a Roman epitaph. Their pleasures, obvious and inexpensive, were those of German peasants; and in their earnest but undexterous appreciation of literature there was something—yes, that was it!—something almost English. Regnard, for instance, was unintelligible to both doltish tribes; and both would prefer the melancholy of Jacques to that of Alceste.

Lac Léman itself has defects of taste and emphasis, but a short excursion towards the Jura will supply the antithesis of these in ample

31

measure. The road to Ferney (16) is a well-beaten one, and its dust has settled upon many an eminent foot. In 1806, when Benjamin Constant went there, it was already a place of pilgrimage, and he found that Voltaire's old servant was doing her best to ensure that, in death as in life, her master should be controversial matter. She felt sure that he had been poisoned; but she herself died soon afterwards, and when, in 1837, Sainte-Beuve paid a devotional call, only an aged gardener remained from the old wizard's twenty-two servants. Nine years later, Flaubert was able to enjoy the house without any distraction. For more than a century now, Ferney has profited by being a truly private house, exempt from the daily erosion of quality and character which is the fate of museums. Even a spell of German occupation could not spoil it; possibly the relics of its sly and cadaverous owner had still some magical power to dissolve stupidity and pride.

From the French frontier the road stretches ahead through fields very like the flattest, wettest part of Leicestershire. Nothing can be seen of Ferney village, and the route has no landmarks, except perhaps a derelict motor-coach from which thrifty persons have removed the wheels, upholstery and lamps. As one approaches the town, the first traces of Voltaire's beneficence appear; for one could say of him that he found Ferney wattle and left it brick. Most of its houses were built by him; and where there had been a wretched hamlet of mindless peasants, he quickly created a prosperous small town, whose craftsmen worked to order for customers from London to Bengal. At the château itself he worked from five in the morning until ten in the evening, while superfluous towers were razed and walls of clipped hornbeam planted in their place. Marble was brought by water across the lake, and he gave special attention to his experimental stud-farm. He saw himself as, variously, a blind mole, a shepherd out of Hesiod, a husbandman on leave from the Georgics, and an old rat withdrawn from the world in the recesses of a Swiss cheese. He built a church and a theatre and several pleasure-houses —pavilions worthy of Meudon and Saint-Cloud. He lay in bed until noon, and he halved the price of salt.

As one turns off the main road and walks up to the house, other English visitors come to mind—Mr. Sherlock, for instance, librarian to the Earl of Bristol. He called in the spring of 1776, and found his host in "a grizzle-wig with three ties" and a silk nightcap embroidered in gold and silver. When they went out into the garden, Voltaire had on shoes of white cloth, white woollen stockings and red breeches, with a nightgown and waistcoat of blue linen, flowered and lined with yellow. He claimed that his garden was in the English taste. In his excitement Sherlock forgot much of the talk, but when he got back to his inn he did remember that the old man had "said some shocking things against Moses and Shakespeare". In the library, Voltaire was at pains to show the range of his English reading. "Robertson is your Livy," he suddenly asserted; and "Addison's *Cato* is incomparably well written ". Horace Walpole's *Historic Doubts* had been well thumbed, but in Bolingbroke Voltaire found "many leaves, and little fruit"; from Roscommon, on the other hand, he quoted from memory the provocative couplet:

> *The weighty bullion of one sterling line,*
> *Drawn to French wire, would through whole pages shine.*

The great patron of the alexandrine remarked, too, that the English in their speech were "energetic, precise and barbarous". And while the liveried footmen carried in the silver and the plate, Voltaire resumed his attacks upon Shakespeare—"a man who would do anything to get money".

The French of Beaumarchais is still spoken at Ferney; and by this musical speech, as much as by the portraits of Clairon and Lekain which still hang on the walls of Voltaire's bedroom, one is reminded of his passion for the theatre and for the great extensions and elaborations of language for which the stage gives occasion. The best actors of a great age for the theatre excelled themselves in Voltaire's rôles; within living memory Salvini made a success of *Zaire*, and Turgenev knew long speeches from the plays by heart; but to-day his plays seem stiff and cold, and we can hardly picture the discipular zeal with which Gibbon, among many others, would race across country to see them performed. There was something of snobbery in these audiences, something of sociability, and something of a pious or morbid wish to hear the aged poet cackling his way, perhaps for the last time, through *Alzire* or *Zulime*. For Voltaire himself they were pure carnival. There was nothing he enjoyed more; and it was with, at most, a false gesture of regret that he reached for the cothurnus and the buskin. "The children and the neighbours" were his excuse, and the agreeable stir of homage his reward. In August 1763, when he played Genghis-Khan in *L'Orphelin de la Chine*, he was an old man, and could pardonably have been a tired one. He had been immoderately active all summer; a case of Popish injustice had taken up much of his time; his eyes troubled him; he had been busy stoking up Marmontel's claim to a vacant place in the Académie; and his dramatic ambitions allowed him no peace. In twelve days he had knocked off a tragedy of Roman life. Full of coarse realism, in "the English taste", it shirked none of the implications of Augustus's epigram, which begins:

> *Quod futuit Glaphyram Antonius, hanc mihi poenam*
> *Fulvia constituit, se quoque uti futuam.*

Le Triumvirat had all the elements, he thought, of a Drury Lane success; for French audiences some pruning might be needed. There was, among the hundred-odd visitors who came to hear *L'Orphelin de la Chine*, a person of Mongolian origin who assured Voltaire that he and Genghis-Khan were as alike as two peas, and that his gestures had been in the true Tartar style. He was delighted with this tribute and repeated it to those who remained to supper, and afterwards danced until four o'clock in the morning. Among the trophies of Ferney—the portraits of Frederick the Great and Catherine of Russia, the busts of Newton and Locke, the copies of Italian masters and the porcelain stove—is the circlet of laurel with which Voltaire was crowned on his last visit to Paris. *Irène*, the pretext for this homage, has now fallen out of the repertory, and at Ferney the theatre has been pulled down and the church has the air of a drill-hall far gone in disuse; but the house itself, and the neat acres of the property, have even on a wet Sunday the prestige and the shimmering excitement of a great staging-point in the history of intelligence.

Coppet (19) has, over Ferney, advantages of rank and favour. Necker spared no expense which might dignify his chosen ark; his barns are big enough for Gloucestershire, and on his roofs the tiles have ripened like peaches. The house itself is recognizably a country house, but with the formality, the well-spaced, well-shuttered windows and the ceremonious chimney-stacks of a Parisian hotel of the period. Flights of gates, with good ironwork and substantial piers, lead the eye inwards; and on the garden front the sweet roundness of a feudal tower has been absorbed into the general idea of a great Minister's seat. To-day everything at Coppet has, in larger measure, the quality remarked by Sainte-Beuve in 1837—that of a little Versailles bereft of its fêtes; its grasses are taller, its waters more glassy, and the shade of its walks deeper and more cobwebby than ever. It is easy to bring to the house and its park the ears of Fauré or the eyes of Hubert Robert—easier perhaps than to describe it with the voice of Proust, and to murmur aside that "il est exquis d'arriver à Coppet par une journée amortie et dorée d'automne, quand les vignes sont d'or sur le lac encore bleu". . . . Nothing now disturbs the long farewell of its overgrown alleys, and there is little to suggest that the deserted house was once a cock-pit for the best intelligences of

19   Mme de Staël's Château at Coppet (1767-71)

20   Byron's Villa Diodati at Cologny

21   Gibbon's summer house at Lausanne

22   Rousseau and Mme de Warens at Les Charmettes

Europe; one can lie for hours in the long grass without courting the fate of Gætano Catruffo who, while similarly engaged, found himself the uneasy spectator, at three paces, of a quarrel such as his hostess alone knew how to conduct. Catruffo, by profession a composer of Maltese opera buffa, may well have felt nervous indoors, for the routine of the day was remote from Mediterranean convention. The first general meal was taken at eleven in the morning, and thenceforward Madame de Staël drew without mercy upon the talent and experience of her guests until midnight when, in the words of one regular guest, "one either went to bed, or one had to go on talking". At table the chatelaine would direct the conversation with the aid of a newly-cut twig from the garden. Once in play with this leafy baton, she would defer only to her father; other men could fight their way out. It is difficult now to recapture the tremors with which men made their way into her company. Much must be added, for instance, to the posthumous portrait by Gérard; and Madame Lebrun's version, with its lyre-bird motif, must have seemed odd to those who had endured Madame de Staël's furious dissection of political subjects. By some surplus of magic, she imposed herself as the woman of the age; this she achieved equally in the case of those who knew her intimately and of those who, many years later, found that her behaviour during the Revolution was that of a heroine of ancient times. Even the Duke of Wellington, who must have advanced towards her a breast-work of the hardest teak, admitted that "she was a most agreeable woman, if you only *kept her light*, and away from politics". The sustained masculinity of her talk was balanced, in intimate relations, by coquetry upon a prodigious scale. The advance and withdrawal of her affections was marked by terrible disputes. Benjamin Constant records how he had to wait, almost as if in a queue, until at one or two in the morning he could get in to have his turn. No man, it is clear, could ever take her father's place; Constant would eye with mounting irritation the extraordinary zoo which gathered every evening to pay homage to the woman who might have been, among other things, the consort of the younger Pitt. Her family had missed, indeed, a connection with more than one great Englishman; but Madame de Staël seemed not to regret this. She and Constant saw Gibbon with the eyes of a younger, post-Revolutionary generation. They got out his letters to her mother and laughed together at what seemed to them the affected and ridiculous style of his love-making; the element of purposeful refrigeration is perhaps more obvious to us. When she looked at Gibbon she wondered if she would ever have sprung from such curious loins, and decided that Necker alone could have brought off the feat. Gibbon himself was not above judging his hosts at Coppet, and took comfort from the poor ruined piece of political humanity who pottered inconsolably about his demesne. "With all the means of private happiness in his power," he wrote to Sheffield, "he is the most miserable of human beings." And Coppet has retained some trace of the ennui, the weight of sad comparisons with which it was loaded both by Necker and by his daughter. The natural beauties of the scene were nothing to her; and on her walks by the lake one may feel sure that, if pleased at all, she was

> *Pleased rather with some soft ideal scene,*
> *The work of Fancy—*

and one can even guess its location. When she was in exile and forbidden to approach within a wide radius from Paris, she would dart angrily from one perimeter-town to another—from Auxerre to Châlons, from Blois to Saumur—until at last she dared to hide in Paris itself, coming out only at night to walk along the moonlit streets.

Madame de Staël had learnt as a young girl the art of mastering herself with the help of the classical authors. Cato (in Addison's translation), Tacitus and Plutarch had saved her from any extremity of despair during the Revolution; and during the years at Coppet—relatively the slackwater of her life—theatrical ventures provided the greatest release for her energies. A pupil of Clairon, she could incarnate, in the tragedies of Voltaire and Racine, all the largeness of sentiment and the animal vitality of which nobody, in so-called "real life", had been able to take full charge. Thus Coppet, as much as Ferney, became a house of rendezvous for connoisseurs of acting. Others besides the Phèdre or the Hermione of the evening took pleasure in the work; Constant, for instance, looked forward to the objurgations which fell to him as Zopire in *Mérope*. People would stand for seven hours in the narrow library for the privilege of watching so curious a scene. A century of Broglies and Haussonvilles has since given to Coppet the savour of a polite and learned society—a world in which, as Proust was pleased to compute, the Princesse de Beauvau and the Comtesse de Talleyrand would motor over from Lausanne, the Princesse de Caraman-Chimay would come from Amphion and the Comtesse Greffulhe would stop for an hour on her way to Lucerne. But a solitary winter-visitor might pause in the flagged hall and seem to overhear, in the adjoining room, the accents in which, through the intermediary of Racine, Madame de Staël echoed the secret of an earlier seductress. "C'est moi, Prince," she is saying—and with the words she leads us down to the inmost zone of her being:

C'est moi dont l'utile secours
Vous eût du Labyrinthe enseigné les détours.

Racine's labyrinth is known to us now as a warren of sexual tunnels, the more terrifying for the posed deliberation of his narrative; but we need not follow Madame de Staël as, swathed in her statutory purple, she crosses its boundary; for our own present pleasures we have to tread more kindly mazes.

Only the *train-omnibus* stops at Coppet, but the high-road through the little town bears throughout the year a frieze of *café-au-lait* roadsters, hot and tarry from their chase along the open country between Geneva and Lausanne. The train is perhaps better suited to this shelving orchard-country. From its open windows one can watch the revolving hoses cast rainbows, in the shape of a scythe or an hourglass, above lawns of English perfection; and one glimpses the watery parks in which lie houses such as Prangins and Doregny, houses embalmed in the lavender and verbena of the First Empire; on the higher slopes, beneath the wooded Jura, the parks have other features—deserted bell-towers, fountains and terraces which step down through rich, well-cultivated land. By the lake are tiny harbours, built like the pincers of a crab, each with its arbour of plane-trees, cropped umbrella-wise. This is good country for schools, and in the hills above the lake tubby belles, the pride of Didsbury and Edgbaston, totter from the ping-pong table to the swimming-pool, or construe passages from Romains and Duhamel.

The north shore of Lac Léman has now the aspect of almost uninterrupted parkland. In summer a hot sun softens the dangerous road from Geneva to Lausanne, and in the streets of Nyon and Morges the wireless-wands of the Packards and the Cadillacs are thick as masts in Brixham estuary. Most of the big houses along the lake lie hidden behind inviolable screens of foliage, and only occasionally does a scarlet umbrella or the striped awning of an electric yacht betray the desirable life which one must suppose, however rashly, to be led along these shores. For it is here, if anywhere, that those artful and splendid survivors, the Emperor-moths of Western civilization, can still enjoy the eternal July of their leisured existence. Or perhaps they can't, after all; for this fondness for the water's edge is of fairly recent origin, and many householders may now regret the purchase of mansions which may only be inhabited with pleasure for a few months in the year. The decisive and tonic unpleasantness of an English winter would seem a continual pleasure-party if compared with the damp lid of fog and cold which shuts down on Lac Léman from October to March. Yet even in bad weather an English visitor will be pleased to find, as perhaps nowhere else in Switzerland, that the country consists mostly of large estates each with its appropriate Seat.

The Seat has, even in democratic times, a considerable importance in English country life. The ancient hierarchy of Doctor's house, Rectory, Manor-house and Seat has not quite been broken down. The nineteenth century, and above all the eleven volumes of Neale's *Views*, mark, however, the zenith of the concept. The poet's eye was then as active as the engraver's needle. Who can forget Crabbe's placing of his Gentleman Farmer? This thoughtful concubinary had a drawing-room "whose sofas rose in bold elastic swell". "His taste was gorgeous," Crabbe tells us, "but it still was taste." Small wonder, then, that

His rooms were stately, rather fine than neat,
And guests politely called his house a Seat.

Large private estates are not common in Switzerland. Nor, among the Swiss themselves, is that "temporary retirement of the opulent" which it was the privilege of the Seat, in Neale's view, to make possible. Feudal strongposts, rather, are the regular ornament of Swiss landscape. Along the north shore of the Lake of Neuchâtel there are admittedly some Seats on the English model, and in time we shall inspect them, masked though they may be by dripping evergreens, a winding gravel drive and a formal notice "Beware of the Dog". Meanwhile, the Pays de Vaud can show Seats of every sort.

Earlier and wiser generations set their houses well back from the water's edge. Apart from anything else, high ground was less vulnerable. At Vufflens, for instance, a mile or two above Morges, the château is a fortified palace of the early fifteenth century. Country life and garrison life, as Pierre Grellet has remarked, begin to be separated at Vufflens; but, for all that, the great central donjon has four smaller towers to supplement it, each with its apparatus of defence. Vufflens is original also in being built of brick, a material disregarded by the stone-hewing builders of Grandson and Chillon. Now that we have almost forgotten the natural éclat of brickwork, and the outline of Vufflens resembles at a distance the ambitions of a Scottish railway hotel, it is difficult to recapture the effect of daring and assurance which the castle must once have inspired. Vufflens must be seen from within. Only then can one really appreciate the

insolent composure of this armoured cliff; only then will its promontories, its fortified ledges assume their original grandeur; only
then we can judge of how the Savoyards could afford, in their years
of triumph, to duplicate for decoration's sake the features which,
elsewhere in the house, marked the points at which an invader
would turn and fly. For some three centuries a single family has
owned this castle, and through their care the rib-vaulted cells of the
fifteenth century exist side by side with *dessus-de-portes* in the style
of Tiepolo; one may picture also the visit of the Empress Josephine
to Vufflens in 1810.

It was in the autumn of 1810 that the repudiated Empress first
visited the Pays de Vaud. Imperious by nature and by habit, the
Empress imposed her visits upon even the most retiring of landowners. At Vufflens the flowers enchanted her, and the view from
the balcony; she herself must, however, have been the most memorable of sights, dressed as she was in a long-sleeved and high-necked
dress of sky-blue levantine, a long overcoat lavishly frogged with
gold, a hat of blue feathers and a yellow silk scarf. Before long she
was herself a householder, having acquired the seat of Pregny-la-
Tour. Two years later, when she took up residence there, the general
promiscuity of her manners was still allied to an unseemly and inappropriate style of dress. It was soon put about that she never refused
an invitation. Curiosity, rather than respect, was the motive of her
hosts; and when they were invited back, they were surprised to find
that, so far from emulating the glacial civilities of Genevese convention, the Empress required them to join in a programme of nursery
games from which even Kiss-in-the-ring was not excluded. One
observer was pleasantly affected by the sight of her head-dress,
executed as this was in the Chinese fashion, with large silver ornaments strewn among the strands of hair (these, he remarks, were
"collected together on the occiput"); and on her forehead and throat
were still larger embellishments of silver, which flashed and glittered
to a great distance. Conversation with her had the further sensational
hazard that she was often pleased to utter unguardedly the most
fearful, unrepeatable calumnies. One may picture the plight of many
a grave senior when the Imperial finger incised upon his forehead
(advanced, like a plate of molten wax, for the favour of some banal
inscription) the print of some unmentionable charge against the
Emperor. Her visit was as memorable as it was brief, but few of her
new acquaintances were sorry to see her go; as one of them remarked:
"The kind of life that we have led since she has been here is not at
all suited to our normal habits." As often happens, however, the
common people were more sensitive to warmth and openness of

heart than were those whose concept of gentility forbade them to acknowledge these qualities. One may read for example in Mrs. Jameson's *Diary of an Ennuyée* of the regard in which the Empress was held by her boatman—the servant also, in his time, of Byron.

It is not far from Vufflens to Aubonne. A few miles, at most, of opulent and umbrageous parkland, with here and there lesser Seats; these are most often locked and bolted, for autumn, winter and enlivening spring find their owners always in town-houses at Morges, Nyon or Rolle. At Aubonne we must disregard Dr. Jenny's casual "Casino, 1850" in order to scrutinize the château. This has for its dominant feature a high round tower, topped by a tapering red cap. This unambiguous erection was restored in the late seventeenth century, when Aubonne belonged to the celebrated traveller J. B. Tavernier. Aubonne seemed to Tavernier the nearest to Eden of all terrestrial sights. Nor did he come lightly to his decision. Tavernier had seen nearly every curious spectacle the world could offer, from the ruins of Babylon to the waterlogged prairie of the Sargasso Sea, from the splendours of court life in Warsaw and Vienna to the dismembered temple of Ephesus. To them all, he preferred Erivan in Persia. Rich pastures, and the near eminence of Mount Ararat, provided a fertile and various background for the stately encounters in which Tavernier would issue forth from his scarlet pavilion to do business with the great persons of the neighbourhood. To the pleasures of venery were added those of the table: pomegranates and the super-excellent melons of Persia were there in abundance. Aubonne would seem to have reminded him, however distantly, of Erivan; and in 1670 he bought the barony of the neighbourhood, began to decorate the château in the Oriental style, and commenced author. He lived for fifteen years at Aubonne, and saw the recital of his voyages become one of the most fashionable and influential books of the age.

It is easy, in this rolling countryside, to become agreeably lost, and, on sighting the Seats of the eighteenth century, to imagine oneself back in the unblemished Arcadia which we glimpse in the pastoral diaries of the period or in the engravings of Engelmann. Let us take one of these engravings. It is August and the covered terrace of this country house is drowsing in afternoon sun. Potted plants are disposed along the balustrade, and sofas, chairs and a corner-cupboard have been brought out in acknowledgment of high summer. The drawing-room windows are closed and shuttered against the glare. On the most comfortable of the sofas the lady of the house is sitting. Book and inkwell lie unheeded before her. What can be holding her attention? Not, we may be sure, the unassertive landscape and the pond-smooth lake. She is thinking, in this last decade before the French Revolution, of the innocent pleasures of life in the Vaud. She takes up her pen. "To-day", she writes, "is July 1st, 1787. I am alone in the country, and enjoying a peace which I should like to fix for ever in my heart. The tranquillity of everything around me contributes something to it, as does the withdrawal from town life, where one becomes involved, willy-nilly, in the passions of others. . . ." Catherine de Sévéry was thirty-four at that time, and had had cause to speak with feeling on such topics, and to wish for her children only such happiness as she was now enjoying—"a countryside agreeable in itself, far enough from the town to deter the false and the indolent, and yet near enough to have news, books, provisions and from time to time a few people whose company gives one pleasure. The really enjoyable way to see one's friends is to have in one's house two or three people at a time—people who enjoy books and the country, who spend the morning walking, or in their rooms, meet for dinner in perfect liberty and in the evening play some game or other. For all this one needs people who are equable, not at all jealous, and delighted by the prospect of enjoying a pretty landscape, even if it doesn't belong to them. Such people are found in France, but not in Switzerland."

At such moments Madame de Sévéry aspired never to leave her property. Even in December, she thought, life would be tolerable, with "every possible book, horses to ride, a gig for visiting, sleighs in wintertime, a good dinner each evening, games to suit every taste; and good health, and health's familiar—gaiety". This tranquil, eventless gaiety was real, moreover. Many are the witnesses who testify to the day-long picnics in hay-strewn orchards, the afternoons with *Clarissa* and *La Nouvelle Héloïse* in plane-arbours saturated with October sunlight, the piquet after supper and the long cross-country drives to see a friend. Astronomy, village dances and the visits of Italian singers diversified the summer round; ideal domestics were matured, like old brandy, by sixty years of careful handling; and, for the members of the Order of St. Hubert, there was hunting. Women, in general, did not hunt; but even the most delicate would put down their novels and run with pleasure to where, behind their hedge of juniper-trees, hounds were pouncing on the hare. Sometimes there were more formal amusements. At Saint-Sulpice, near Lausanne, the little eleventh- or twelfth-century church, of Cluniac foundation, has now for its neighbours a petrol-station, a hippodrome and a manufactory of funeral sculpture, but there is still, by the lake, a leafy, sandy avenue where horsemen pass. It is holy ground, moreover, for Bonapartists; for on the flat ground nearby, Napoleon reviewed in 1800 the army which was to distinguish itself at Marengo. But a less virile occasion now claims our attention. It was at St. Sulpice, in the little wooded promontory which gives on to the lake, that the most elaborate of Vaudois entertainments was given. Reputedly a frog-infested jungle of briars, the wood lent itself perfectly to the occasion. A slight *bise* kept the air fresh and cool, and at noon the large company repaired, each in his best, to the farthest depths of the little forest. A large table had been laid with chocolate, coffee and cream; and when the Duchess of Württemberg had arrived, with six horses to draw her carriage, musicians were seen to be approaching by water. Each lady was next presented with a bouquet by the children of the host and hostess—a ceremony which lasted until three o'clock. Dinner was then served; with the band (not a very good one) braying away in the distance, a certain familiar gaiety began to envelop the scene. Dancing followed. *Allemandes, contredanses* and *rondes* occupied the company until, at a given signal, all moved off to the lakeside and there embarked in ornamental barges. Of course there were hazards in so vast a venture, but they were of a mild sort. One guest wrote afterwards, "I was so weak as to dance with Barral, and I regretted it when he began biting and kissing my fingers; I took care to keep him at a distance, but he succeeded, none the less, in taking certain liberties." But such annoyances are not lasting, and when the same witness came to collate her memories of the day, she could hardly contain her delight. "What impressed me most," she wrote, "was the sight of so many carriages and so many liveried servants, all mixed up in the middle of a wood with people from St. Sulpice, the poor and their children, a lot of sheep and cows, and the fine ladies and gentlemen—all together and arranged among the branches in groups so various and extraordinary that I should have liked to paint them, every one."

It is from recollections of this sort, as much as from the frenzied imaginings of Byron, Rousseau and Shelley, that Lac Léman has come to be associated with the idea of happiness. Not that one should exaggerate: the châtelaines of 1780 found, as their successors do today, that "apathy, boredom and desiccation" are the certain results of too long a period of rusticated leisure. The weather then, as now, inclined to inconvenient extremes; there were epidemics of dysentery, and once even a plague of mad foxes. But, all the same, the parklands of the Vaud must always represent, for those who know them, the image of an ideal contentment.

As the train passes behind Morges, with its Louis XVI church and part-time hippodrome, it is agreeable to recall that this landscape can still act as nursemaid to great enterprises. For at Morges, in

1918, Stravinsky and C. F. Ramuz composed that pocket masterpiece, *L'Histoire du Soldat*. Ramuz is of course the veteran laureate of the area, but Stravinsky has also an old allegiance to the Léman; in 1908, while walking along its banks, he conceived the idea of *Petrouchka*; later he worked with Ravel at Clarens and with Diaghilev at Lausanne; and in 1918, in a time of penury and distress, he had grafted on to a fable of Afanasiev the precise and exacting score of the *Soldat*. Directed, as always, by Ernest Ansermet, this unique entertainment is sometimes revived at Lausanne. On such occasions the tiny band is placed, as Stravinsky decrees, upon the stage, and its members surmount, with varying degrees of equanimity, the prodigious hardships of their task. As for the illustrious chef (I owe to the *Gazette de Lausanne* this just, if at first baffling, appellation)— only by an occasional scratch at his leg does he suggest that the score may be more difficult than that of "Let's All Go To the Ball-Game".

Lausanne itself is holy ground for literary persons. Gibbon's *berceau* (21) has gone for ever, but many streets and houses known to him may still be traced, and there is even the possibility, most enticing to literary truffle-hounds, of finding in some *antiquaire* a book from his library. Of his attachment to the town it would be impertinent for me to speak had not a Swiss scholar freshly illumined the subject by giving us the full text of the *Lausanne Journals*. Nor is Lausanne, in general, a town for nostalgia. The Lausannois is too intent upon the present, too pleased with the transient bloom of health which gives even the plainest Swiss girl a moment of attraction; to the visitor the life of the town appears uniformly brisk. The funicular climbs up and down in its pebbly trough; on the tennis-courts green-visored professionals are for ever breaking into another box of balls from Slazenger's; oarsmen, bicyclists, ski-ers and *basketteurs enragés* comprise nearly all the adult population. Peak-capped undergraduates enhance the scene; and unless, like Charles-Albert Cingria, one explores the low quarters of the town in search of the underground source of the Flon, one may fancy that the heart of Lausanne is in the gymnasium, or in the delicious confectioner's in the rue de Bourg, or in the dogs' cemetery which lies beneath the ancient cedars of the Beau-Rivage. At Nyffenegger's a select public nibbles its *foie-gras* sandwiches or hovers above the strawberry tarts which have been flown, this very morning, from somewhere south of the Alps. Down by the lake, in the quarter given over, as Cingria says, to cinders, swans and railway-lines, it is possible for English visitors to sit undisturbed, sampling the wine of the neighbourhood; this harmless reversion to Byronic practice may, moreover, provoke the tourist to brood contentedly upon the many-lustred history of Lausanne's contribution to European literature.

In Loudon's *Encyclopædia of Gardening* the opinion is ventured that "a great part of the Pays de Vaud is like the best part of Berkshire". This can never have been true of the view from Gibbon's *berceau* of acacias, and it is not true to-day of the *berceau* itself, since this was replaced in 1901 by a monumental post office in the style of Louis XIII. From December to March it is difficult to get in or out of this building, or to station oneself in front of it, without damage from the picks, axes, runners and spikes of the winter-sportsman. In Gibbon's time the mountains were politely and justly ignored by the cosmopolitan society of Lausanne; faro, gossip and private theatricals were their normal employments at this season; but to-day the collective porcupine of ski-ers enjoys pre-eminence. "Not with a bang, but a Whymper" should be the English blazon of these formidable persons. Softer tastes have recently been indulged, however, by the publication of the full text of Gibbon's *Lausanne Journals*. These were written in French; they cover the later period, from August 1763 to April 1764, of his second visit to Switzerland; and they have been edited on the spot, with all possible care, by Professor Bonnard.

Gibbon was twenty-six when, in May 1763, he re-crossed the Swiss border. Lausanne was then, as now, the rendezvous for a thoughtful and animated society of Swiss, and an international society of exiles. These jointly became Gibbon's companions. Among them he could shine at his ease, while in an adjoining room the blubbering boys and the knicker-hungry Guardees bickered sullenly around the billiard-table. Ten years had transformed him. No longer did he sit speechless, a disgraced undergraduate, at the parsonical table of Monsieur Pavilliard. The world had claimed him, and he had claimed the world. "It appears", he noted in his *Journal*, "that the Prince of Württemberg has a great liking for me. He has an easy and natural politeness for everyone, but with me he adopts a tone of confidence, of esteem, and almost of affection." The Lausanne notebooks may not be among their author's Lapidaria, and indeed M. Bonnard lists a number of battles, atrocious but decisive, between himself and the grammar, syntax and orthography of the diarist. The Gibbonian forefinger was none the less raised as effectively in French as in English, and never more so than in describing the human curiosities of the town. His reading offered, in relation to these, a series of prompt, if involuntary, parallels. From the *Third Satire of Juvenal* he learnt how quickly a plain and pious people may be debauched by the amenity of foreign manners. In November, when the first layers of snow had fallen upon Lausanne, he discovered, from the *Travels in Greenland* of the Danish traveller Hans Egede, that even in the Arctic Circle certain simple pleasures could still be enjoyed. *"Oui,"* he noted, *"l'homme est naturellement bon! J'en appelle à ces Groenlandois, qui connaissent l'amour au milieu de leurs frimas. . . ."* The eternal snows of Chimborazo and the discreet withdrawal ("two yards every hundred years") of the sea from the coastline of Sweden offered further points of interest to a visitor who perforce gazed daily on the Dents du Midi and the variable delta of the Rhône.

Scrutiny of Nardini and Cluvcrius persuaded him for the moment that "the geographer sees, perhaps better than the historian, what it cost the universe to become Roman"; but when he looked at his companions in Lausanne, it was with a more than geographical eye. A few elderly and distinguished Swiss were alone admitted to rank with himself. Monsieur de Chandieu-Villars, who had spent his life in the French Army, was one of these—"a man of great politeness, with an easy and lively intelligence . . . almost the only foreigner who has acquired the smoothness of French manners without at the same time giving himself noisy and idiotic airs". Intellectuals had not this facility, and of poor Woest, the faithful philosophical chopping-block of Gibbon's restless hours, the diarist remarked that "one may discern his nationality from the coarseness of his manners". One man, however, did he absolutely detest: Colonel Juste Constant, who "unites in his person even those bad qualities which are most remote from each other—grossness and artifice, malice and stupidity, avarice and prodigality. He is in effect *Monstrum nulla virtute redemptum."* The allusion to Juvenal's great attack on Crispinus ("a sickly creature, vigorous only in debauch") may have solaced Gibbon for the tiny slights and distresses which Constant inflicted upon him; in these he would seem to have shown a dexterity worthy of the nobler causes to which his son Benjamin later devoted himself.

The English themselves were very mixed. There were decent, studious and inhibited travellers like Lord Palmerston, and ill-conditioned beasts like Sidney. There was the amiable and alcoholic Guise, and Captain Clarke, the retired Naval man. There was John Holroyd, later to become the dearest of Gibbon's friends, and there was Mr. Beckford, the author not of *Vathek* but of *Thoughts on Hare and Fox-Hunting*. There was Mr. Shuttleworth: *"qu'il faudra du savon pour le décrasser"*; and there were the anonymous others who, while Gibbon was deciphering Spanheim and Vossius at his desk above the Léman, would vex him with the clicking of their billiard-balls, and later turn his rooms into their habitual café. Had these

45

been all, he must have been very discontented; but there were also such dependable friends as Saussure and Deyverdun; and there were the ladies.

While in no sense an amorist, Gibbon was a flirt. The air, if not the fact, of sex was indispensable to his existence. Like Stendhal, he was enraptured by the phenomenon, common to both Lausanne and Geneva, of the unmarried young girls (exemplary vestals, moreover) who went everywhere unchaperoned, and offered to the goatish pretensions of travelling Englishmen a resistance as effective as it was delicate. Gibbon was happy with them, and enjoyed, too, the dwindling but still potent attractions of his former attachment, Mademoiselle Curchod. Can it be by coincidence, however, that during the first week of February he made the acquaintance both of Madame de Seigneux and of Ovid's account, in the *Fasti*, of the Floral Games of ancient Rome? He was experiencing at that time one of those rebounds of animal interest which often accompany the check or dismissal of more elevated appetites. He had not prospered in society as much as he would have wished; there had been a rebuff at the Cercle (the White's of Lausanne); he had been dropped from houses at which the Prince of Württemberg dined; the senior personages of the town no longer showed him, he complained, "that respect, those flattering distinctions upon which I used to count". He was reduced, in fact, to enjoying the weather. At this low point in his fortunes he went to a party at which was a youthful but practised enchantress. She was from Aarau, but had married into the first society of Lausanne. "Not pretty," Gibbon noted, "but with a vivacity, and a rumpled and mutinous manner, which render her very interesting. She always grasps one's meaning, never takes offence, and replies in the same tone. What temperament she has! There is an evident and very decided lubricity in her eyes, her gestures, and everything she says. For this reason they had to marry her off at the age of fifteen, because . . ." Warmed by this new acquaintance, and stirred by Ovid's explicit though glacial narrative, Gibbon noted on the following day that "the flower-season has always aroused licentious ideas . . . even in men who were very certainly ignorant of the story of the courtesan Flora".

It came to nothing, of course. After seven weeks of delicious manœuvring for wind and station, Gibbon broke a new signal; "disengage" read the flags at his masthead. A week or two more and he had left Lausanne for Italy.

Intellectually, his visit had been a success. He had gained, moreover, in knowledge of the world. He had been interested, though not implicated, in a prosecution for disorderly conduct; he had averted a duel between two friends; he had taken lessons in French declamation; he had been cupped. Yet there were things which rankled, and as he left Lausanne for the second time he confessed to disappointment. Where once he had seen a paradise, he now saw "a town, ill-built in a delightful landscape, which enjoys peace and quietude, and mistakes them for liberty. . . . Affectation is the original sin of the Lausannois. Affectation of wealth, nobility and intelligence—the first two being very common and the third very rare." Did there rise before him at this point a lubricious but inaccessible image? He turned, at any rate, and with outstretched forefinger continued: "Their love of ostentation accords ill with their taste for nobility; yet they would die rather than renounce it or embrace the only profession which would allow them to keep it up."

Such ungallantry is, of course, a thing of the past; but very similar strictures have been levelled, in recent years, at Lausanne itself. Ramuz, for one, called it "une ville qui a tourné mal"; and many less famous but equally vigilant writers have deplored the fact that within the last hundred years Lausanne has lost or abused, not only the charm which endeared it to Gibbon, but the unique advantages of its physical position. Even the casual visitor may see for himself that the process is by no means completed, as one by one the older houses of the delinquent city are laid in ruins to make way for the imbecile erections of our own time. For Lausanne is not one of those places— and they are many in Switzerland—in which the old has been replaced by the genuinely new. In so far as these accretions look anywhere, they look backward; and meanwhile the city, which might have been disposed in memorable terraces above a memorable inland sea, has been allowed to peter out in streets which nowhere acknowledge the grandeurs of the site.

At what point, one wonders, did the delectable hill-town of Gibbon's recital begin to go wrong? Ramuz plumps for the year in which *La Nouvelle Héloise* was first published, and "an unknown little country became, for hundreds of readers, the centre of the world". Certain it is that by 1830 the old town was losing its savour. The six storeys of the Hôtel Gibbon already dominated the Petit-Chêne; beneath, gardens had been arranged with serpentine walks, in the English manner. The 1830s were dignified, none the less, by the sojourn of Sainte-Beuve as visiting lecturer at the Académie de Lausanne. As a monument of literary art, *Port Royal* can stand (and of how many history-books could as much be said?) with *The Decline and Fall of the Roman Empire*; and one cannot sufficiently honour the small town (the size, at that date, of Abingdon or Blandford), which proved itself able, not merely to nourish the phenomenon in its midst, but to estimate it at its true worth. (London University, for example, showed no such insight when, in 1828, Sainte-Beuve offered himself in a tutorial capacity.)

Sainte-Beuve had no physical advantages as a lecturer. Eye-witness accounts of his aspect and demeanour are uniformly unflattering. We are remote, in this context, from the virtuoso-lecturers of our own day. Fry, Wind, Clark have excelled in other ways. Sainte-Beuve was a pallid, half-bald young man, of middle height and with ill-made and irregular features; nor had he any beauty of voice or delivery. Professor René Bray has detailed the stages by which the lecturer rose superior to these handicaps; but what most concerns us here is the faithful tenderness with which Sainte-Beuve regarded the landscape and the people of the Vaud—a tenderness sufficiently indicated in his half-forgotten poems, and in the last lines of his inaugural lecture, where he compares the discreet ardour of the Port-Royalists to the aspect of Lac Léman on an autumn afternoon. "The clouds were such," he said, "that nowhere could I distinguish the sun, or any blue place where the smile of the firmament could break through; but, at a certain part of the lake, and over a certain undefinable zone, I could see, not the image itself of the golden circle, but a refraction, white, dispersed and reflected, of the invisible planet. If one looked from time to time throughout the day, the sky was ever obscured, the golden disc ever invisible; but one could follow the zone of reflected light, the genuine but never dazzling radiance which was making its way along the lake, and remained, for those who cared to watch, a source of reassurance and of consolation." With such delicate compliments did Sainte-Beuve introduce to his hearers the giant figures of Racine, Arnauld, Pascal and Saint-Cyran.

The University itself is now housed for the most part in the Palais de Rumine, a neo-Florentine invention by Louis Bezencenet, whose talents are seen to more advantage in the Hôtel Beau-Rivage at Ouchy. One must dodge behind this palace in order to discover the Académie in which Sainte-Beuve held his class. In this severe and ancient quarter it is possible to recapture the charms to which Gibbon responded; nor should the visitor neglect to climb the covered stairway beloved of Rilke, and to examine the Cathedral and the view from its terrace. Individually, as I have tried to indicate, the buildings of Lausanne are no longer of great merit; but, when seen from a height, they still cohere in impressive fashion. Vast bridges, of Victorian and Edwardian date, emphasize the dramatic basis of the scene; in fine weather the pink and orange stucco of the residential quarters is enlivened with awnings of striped linen; the precipitous rue de Bourg remains, for the glutton, one of the most tempting streets in Europe; and over all is an air of sedate and blameless animation. The Lausannois sit smiling through the ancient Parisian comedies which are brought to their door by French touring companies; smiling, and sometimes even laughing, they scrutinize those ludicrous but affluent beings, the visitors from Egypt and South America. Every season is interesting in Lausanne—from high summer, when the yachts turn the Léman into Dufy's idea of an English regatta, and their tall sails can be seen like white-coated workmen through the foliage of a lakeside garden, right through to Christmas week, when the few foreigners pad silently down the snowy rue St. François, and later gorge as silently in the seclusion of their hotels.

Ouchy to-day is rarely visited for its own sake. People go there to hire a boat, or to get a hair-cut, or to see Mr. Churchill disembark, but they do not stay for any length of time. Still less—I except, of course, the fortunate owners of the mansions which give on to the lake—do they live there. In the nineteenth century this was not yet the case; and a Dickensian souvenir has recently allowed us to penetrate the secrets of life in Ouchy a century ago.

Dickens impressed himself upon many of his Swiss friends, and even after he had left Lausanne he continued, as correspondent, to excite them to unusual efforts of self-expression. A recent memoir informs us, in fact, that one at least of those favoured with his letters habitually gave three full days to the composition of an appropriate reply. One pictures Monsieur de Cerjat at mealtimes, munching his way distractedly through the stuffed lark, the lake trout with anchovy sauce and the tart made with that English novelty, the red-currant; one pictures the hours spent gnawing the quill, and the mark of the agitated thumb upon the rag-paper of palest blue; one pictures the sudden bolt past the chestnuts and through the catalpas to the Napoleonic bathing-house, and thence the immediate plunge into the private harbour. Letter-writing apart, life was very agreeable in the Lausanne of 1855. People never remained for long in one place; those who owned comfortable seats at Ouchy or Doregny habitually wintered at Florence or Pau; failing this, they moved uphill to the neighbourhood of the rue de Bourg, where a score of select shopkeepers worked hard to keep them in tolerable spirits. A simple opulence was the mark of this society, and there were many ingenious devices to prove its sympathy with the English-speaking world. These focused, as was natural, upon the fast-growing English colony; based as this was upon some forty colonels, in retirement from service in Africa and India, its tone was genial but strict; the colonels were great walkers, and the almost perpendicular roadways of Lausanne were an excellent playground for aspiring pedestrians.

British habits obtained throughout the best families of Lausanne. Mothers were tenderly disguised behind pet-names from Walter Scott; *tableaux vivants* culminated in a scene from the *Idylls of the King*; fathers were often to be found reclining on the *canapés Louis Philippe* of the English Lending Library; daughters disputed among themselves for a riding-habit made to measure by Creed, and younger daughters pledged their nascent affections with bracelets of Irish bog-oak. Only when attending Divine Service at the Anglican church did these exemplary young anglophiles step out of character; for then, so the memoir tells us, they wore Algerian burnous of white silk. It was an easy life, among the tulip-trees or the lake-bordering elms; in papa's study the dust never settled upon the many rare birds preserved there under glass; and only a distant tapping, a distant murmuring, revealed that on ground bought from a Miss Allott there were arising the luxurious alcoves of the Hôtel Beau Rivage. Sudden deaths were rare and long remembered: how one young man had met with a fatal accident at a croquet party, and another had fallen, while tipsy, into the bearpit at Berne, and was smothered by the Bruins as he attacked them with his umbrella. Once again it was an English nobleman who alone brought some basic oddity into these temperate lives. Lord Vernon might have moved on, but Lord Radstock more than filled his place. The guest of Monsieur de Shoulepnikow, he had recently returned from Russia, where in the course of an evangelical mission he had founded a seat of Radstockians. A tendency to conclude all his calls with a period of general prayer soon made him conspicuous in Lausanne society, but no conversions were forthcoming in this very level-headed atmosphere. English visitors did not then conform to the miserable norm of our own age. Lord Vernon, for instance, impressed even Dickens (no mean connoisseur of human oddity) by the combination of his tastes. These mated a profound knowledge of Dante with a passion for rifle-shooting. "He has fallen", Dickens noted, "into the strange infatuation of attending every rifle-match in Switzerland, accompanied by two men who load rifles for him, one after another, which he has often been known to fire off, two a minute, for fourteen hours at a stretch, without once changing his position or leaving the ground. He wins all kinds of prizes: gold watches, flags, teaspoons, teaboards, and so forth; and is constantly travelling about with them, from place to place, in an extraordinary carriage, where you touch a spring and a chair flies out, touch another spring and a closet of pickles opens, touch another spring and disclose a pantry. . . ."

There were even English visitors in the 1840s who dared to inhabit the *bas-fonds* of Ouchy, which then had quite a sinister aspect.

23   Solothurn : Fountain of Justice (1561); behind, the Cathedral (1762-63).
Architect, G. M. Pisoni

24 The Château de Chillon

One of these was a baronet, "with a little, loquacious, flat-faced, damaged-featured, *old-young* wife. They delight in a view, and live at Ouchy, down among the drunken boatmen and the drags and omnibuses, where nothing whatever is to be seen but the locked wheels of carts scraping down the uneven, steep, stone pavement." Dickens himself was more comfortably installed at Rosemont, a villa with garden half-way up the hill. Having prudently refused the Elysée, then as now the most seignorial of the lakeside mansions, he lived contentedly in this bowery retreat; took daily walks of up to fifteen miles; was pleasantly disturbed by the news of the town (the drowning of a lovely virgin of seventeen, the escape of a crocodile into the Léman); entertained Thackeray to biscuits and Lieb-fraumilch; began *Dombey and Son*, and first formed the idea of giving public readings.

The Côte de Lavaux is one of the most beautiful prospects in Switzerland; but from Saint-Saphorin onwards a new atmosphere prevails. Even the weather is different. It is warmer, more sedative; the cutting blade of the *bise* is no longer felt. The geometry of the vine is displaced by the softer, leafier outline of the umbrella-plane. Vevey and Montreux are at hand.

Not all visitors, of course, will share my own dislike for these languid resorts. Vevey has still its expiring graces. Only a lout could dislike the Town Hall which, originally built in 1710, was enlarged in 1751. The Cour aux Chantres, built in 1746 for the chatelain of Joffrey, is an imposing town house—or, in Dr. Jenny's excellent phrase, a "majestic horseshoe-erection"; and in the big market-place the Grenette, with its Doric adornments, open market-hall on the ground-floor and massive clock-tower, will remind a sensitive visitor of similar fine buildings at Ledbury and High Wycombe. There are good fountains of the seventeenth, eighteenth and nineteenth centuries, and the Musée Jenisch is agreeably pro-miscuous in its collections. Vevey has always treated foreigners kindly; the graves of Ludlow and Broughton (two of Charles I's judges) will witness to this, and so, in more substantial fashion, does the Russian Church, which was erected in 1878 as the gift of Prince Schouvalow. Admirers of Gogol will be pleased to wander in the town in which *Dead Souls* was begun; and admirers of Rousseau will wish to seek out the Auberge de la Clef. Vevey is at least a genuine town, matured through several centuries of peaceable existence. (To say, as one Swiss writer has done, that it enjoys "an intense anima-tion, untainted by provincialism" is simply to miss the point—as well as to express, one might fairly say, the exact opposite of the truth.) Montreux, by contrast, is a stupid, temporary town, of which nearly every building was run up between 1870 and 1914. Built upon a series of steep slopes, it shows with what ease the amenity of nature may be destroyed by the cupidity of man. The narrow main street, with its multitudinous traffic and slithering trams, has little charm; and unlike the other towns which we have so far discussed, Montreux has nothing interesting to say for itself. It is a pleasure-resort, with all the deserts of ennui and fatuity which that phrase must evoke. It is also a town in which the dominant form of architecture is that of the hotel. Statistics will show why this should be so. In Geneva (assuming every hotel to be full) one person in twenty-nine is a visitor; in Montreux, one person in six In mountain resorts, where visitors sometimes outnumber permanent residents by ten to one, this figure would not be remarkable; but in Montreux it means that the hotels, the pensions and the villas are the buildings which set the style of the town. This does not necessarily make for ugliness; Lugano and Interlaken have the same trait, but were lucky enough to assume it a generation earlier. At Montreux it has not worked happily. The ugliness of Villars and St. Moritz, again, is masked by the inordinate grandeur of the landscape and the brisk, assertive employment of most of the visitors. At Montreux, where people take life very easily, there is time to reflect upon the qualities which elsewhere redeem even such industrial cities as Biel or Winterthur.

The great country house, as I have said, is rare in Switzerland. The ruling class has never attempted, in that country, to seal itself off from the great mass of the people, or to devise for itself a different and superior way of life. It is for this reason that Swiss towns are on the whole so remarkably homogeneous. Between the thirteenth and the fifteenth centuries, Switzerland gradually shook itself free from alien or monarchical influence and a new patriarchy was formed by the guilds—an oligarchy which, in Dr. Peter Meyer's phrase, "was not ashamed to carry on a trade, in addition to the business of state". Except for a period during which the absolutism of the Grand Siècle had some influence upon the wealthier citizens, Swiss public life has remained solidly, indeed splendidly, bourgeois. There was no such thing as an aristocratic architectural style; the guild-houses, town-halls, granaries and market-halls blend in amity with humbler buildings. Style and materials are the same for all. As, moreover, the respect for order and tradition is one of the strongest of Swiss instincts, it is hardly surprising that the aerial photographs to-day so often reveal cities identical in shape and plan with those engraved by Meryan in 1648.

In all this, the hotel has its part. Only after 1850 did greed for gold dictate the design of such inharmonious constructions as now deface the preferred resorts of the foreign visitor. The first palaces retain the charm of an early Murray guide; and as we loiter beneath their heavily moulded cornices, or an assiduous acolyte brings to us, in our wicker armchairs, *The Times* upon its stout wooden pole, it is touching to contemplate the vanished life of the Victorian tourist as he waited, in this very saloon, for the arrival of his Italian cicerone. This life is memorably pictured in the opening paragraph of *Daisy Miller*. A connoisseur of European resorts, and of the fervent but inconclusive attachments which they encourage, Henry James had been quick to remark that Vevey, even then, was a little universe of hotels. "The shore of the lake", he remarks, "presents an unbroken array of establishments of this order, of every category, from the 'grand hotel' of the newest fashion, with a chalk-white front, a hundred balconies and a dozen flags flying from its roof, to the little Swiss pension of an older day, with its name inscribed in German-looking lettering upon a pink or yellow wall and an awkward summer-house in the angle of the garden. One of the hotels at Vevey, however, is famous, even classical, being distinguished from many of its upstart neighbours by an air both of luxury and maturity. In this region, in the month of June, American travellers are extremely numerous; it may be said, indeed, that Vevey assumes at this period some of the characteristics of an American watering-place. . . . There is a flitting hither and thither of 'stylish' young girls, a rustling of muslin flounces, a rattle of dance-music in the morning hours, a sound of high-pitched voices at all times. You receive an impression of these things at the excellent inn of the 'Trois Couronnes' and are transported in fancy to the Ocean House or to Congress Hall. But at the 'Trois Couronnes', it must be added, there are other features that are much at variance with these suggestions: neat German waiters, who look like secretaries of legation; Russian princesses sitting in the garden; little Polish boys walking about, held by the hand, with their governors; a view of the sunny crest of the Dent du Midi and the picturesque towers of the Castle of Chillon."

Chillon is the monument of which it is least easy, at a first glance, to say anything of interest. Originally the lonely and awful guardian of an untenanted shore, it can now be glimpsed only through the cables and gear of an electric railway; kiosks grow wild at its foot; petrol and Chesterfields contribute the characteristic scents of tourism. The legend of Byron and Victor Hugo no longer captivates a generation for whom torture and solitary confinement have been brought out of the footnotes of history. The offshore view of Chillon has been the subject of more bad paintings, one must assert, than any other prospect in the world; even Courbet was beaten by it. All gingerly, therefore, do I proffer the fact that Chillon is one of the most remarkable medieval ensembles in Switzerland; and dowered, moreover, with a history more genial than legend has allowed. Just as it is difficult, while pacing to-day the dilapidated gallery of Chenonceaux, to picture to oneself the abandoned and ambivalent banquet at which Henri III and his catamites were travestied in women's costume, so now at Chillon it is only by a considerable leap of the imagination that one can grasp the splendour and exuberance with which the castle was invested by the rulers of Savoy.

Researches have shown that the rock upon which this castle rests was inhabited even in the Bronze Age. One may turn more profitably, however, to the period from 1150 onwards, when Chillon (already a sizable construction, formerly the property of the Bishops of Sion) came under Savoyard rule. A hundred years later, it had already assumed roughly the shape in which it has endured for seven centuries. The castle remained in Savoyard hands until 1536, when it came under Bernese domination. This lasted until 1733. In 1798 it became Vaudois property, and from 1844 onwards it resumed, though in very much modified style, its function of prison. Pierre Grellet has described this idyllic bondage: "Their main duty was to look after the wine-cellar; this belonged to the kindly and imaginative caretaker who meanwhile conducted visitors round the castle and put fear into them by his lurid anecdotes. His fortunate captives made certain that his wine was properly cool, occasionally swept out the courtyards (by way of civility), fished with rod and line, incised their impressions upon the walls, and renewed the footsteps of Bonivard in order to preserve this valuable historical relic."

This peaceful desuetude is not, perhaps, so stirring to the imagination as the earlier, more brilliant existence of the castle. Chillon is a truly medieval building, in that it sufficed for the whole life of a community. It was a fortified palace, comprising within itself barracks, law-courts, prison, chapel and treasury; and at the foot of the rock would lie the Savoyard galleys, armoured and emblazoned, and each with a hundred oars to regain speed when the wind grew languid and the great lateens hung useless at the mast. In such a context the occasional cruelty of man to his fellows becomes merely one of the eternal rhythms of communal life. This may seem a solemn note on which to leave the Vaud, which could claim at this moment to be the most peaceful countryside in Europe; but it has a bloody history—is it not from regard for the reader's sensibility that I have omitted to evoke the orchards of Grandison, bowed low in 1476 with their harvest of human heads?—and if I have hitherto erred, it has been on the opposite side.

54

25 The Samson
Fountain (1544) (*left*)

26 A view from the
Zeitglockenturn (*right*)]

BERNE

27 Morat

II

Neuchâtel, Berne and the Jura

Neuchâtel—Yverdon—Porrentruy—Payerne—Fribourg—
Gruyères—Berne

ALL Swiss museums are worth a visit, for even in those least
obviously adapted to one's particular taste there is likely to be
at any rate one unpredictable exhibit—the mummified crocodile at Payerne, for instance, or the two-headed cat at Winterthur.
Nowhere is the instinct of motiveless acquisition more evident than
at Neuchâtel; there (one cannot but feel) man and squirrel are one.
The Musée Historique et des Beaux-Arts is hull-down on the lake,
and its entrance-hall has borrowed the calm of those featureless
waters. After a female attendant, tranquil in bearing and clad in a
close-fitting garment of some quilt-like material, has conceded the
right of entrance in return for some trumpery coin, we are made free
of this most singular of collections. In some cases a natural local
pride may be inferred; a series of primitive arrow-heads, for example,
reminds us that at La Tène (not far away, among the marshlands of
the Thiele canal) digging has revealed an important station of the
Iron Age. A large eighteenth-century model of the Hôtel du Peyrou
restores the terraced garden, the contrived wilderness and the groups
of powdered personages who have vanished with the age of Rousseau.
The enthusiast for *vernis martin* will welcome the sight of the
clavichord which, originally built by Ruckers of Antwerp in 1632,
was decorated in the late eighteenth century with scenes from the
Fables of La Fontaine and given by Marie Antoinette to the fiancée
of a Swiss officer who had been killed at the Tuileries. From its long
subjection to the Kings of Prussia, Neuchâtel has retained the portraits of these monarchs from Friedrich Wilhelm I onwards and,
with them, lesser trophies: a snuffbox on which are celebrated the
victories of Friedrich Wilhelm II, a copy of the Great Seal of Prussia,
and an engraving of the scene in which the Prince de Neuchâtel
asked, on Napoleon's behalf, for the hand of Marie-Louise. There
are pretty pieces of silver and glass—seventeenth-century cups in the
likeness of an eagle, a fleur-de-lys and a fir-cone; *verreries du Doubs*
from 1740 to 1820; some of the porcelain stoves by which every
Swiss interior was once ornamented; a cast of Houdon's Rousseau,
and *bonbonnières* of flowered enamel, some of them decorated with

initials in human hair. Baubles from Venice and Bavaria complete the rational side of a survey to which our own century has contributed only a few *art nouveau* spoons. Hitherto we have remarked only those objects to which art, or history, or both, have given an intrinsic charm. The basic tone of the collection is set, however, by case upon case of nineteenth-century flat-irons; broken or incomplete spectacles of the same era compete with the comparative history of the playing-card for the attention of the bemused visitor. Medals of Brazilian origin lie side by side with the bronze key to Lord Wemyss's drawing-room at Basle and a selection of eighteenth-century pharmacy jars. Letters from representative pastors, opticians and geologists are framed beneath a photograph commemorating the Jubilee of the Tir Federal; and the museum as a whole is crowned by the three auto-matons—the writer, the draughtsman and the girl musician—con-structed between 1719 and 1773 by Pierre Jacquet-Droz of La Chaux-de-Fonds and his son Henri-Louis. These beautiful toys can be set in motion for a modest fee. Few buildings, one must assert, can show so wide a range of human curiosity—from the anti-horse traps of the fifteenth century to the gentle trances of Corot and Theodore Rousseau, from Zürich porcelain to the evolution of the harquebus.

Neuchâtel (29) is distinguished from other Swiss towns by a cer-tain ossified elegance. In many of its buildings the yellow sandstone of the neighbourhood has weathered to the colour of the local wines; without going so far as to say, with Alexandre Dumas, that the town looks as if it were carved out of butter, one can assert that it has taken on the colour of October sunshine. Neuchâtel had the good fortune to be the appanage, first of the Dukes of Orléans-Longueville, and later of the Kings of Prussia; proximity to France ensured that even under Prussian domination the town was open to French influence. The whole Quartier de l'Hôpital, for instance, the Hôtel de Ville (built in 1796 by Pierre-Adrien Paris), and, a generation later, the Maison de Pourtalès-Castellane, reflected this influence in cold but faithful style, and it is in character that the town went to a French sculptor, David d'Angers, for the statue of David Purry which now stands, fenced off and bowered in evergreens, in the square which bears his name. But Neuchâtel has a style of its own, with the sharp-ened steeples, or upended prows, of the Halles for its most obvious signatures, and the military fountain of Le Banneret, built in 1581, to recall the distinction with which the Neuchâtelois have fought in the armies of France, Prussia and England—yes, of England, for (as Ogrisek and Rufenacht remind us in their account of the town) a regiment from Neuchâtel took Seringapatam for the East India

Company. The general tone of Neuchâtel—excluding for a moment the specifically French quarters—is one of untroubled provincialism. There is no striving for effect in these uneven streets, where the cobbles seem to have been set by hand and the houses are of the plainest, with here and there some delicate ironwork, a feudal ornament in stone, a flattened First Empire façade of painted wood or (again in the Maison des Halles) an heraldic doorway of the late sixteenth century to push them suddenly into a higher class.

The northern shore of the Lake of Neuchâtel can show many admirable country houses. Set, as often as not, on a slight eminence or overhanging cliff above the lake, with Mont Blanc and the Bernese Oberland as the statutory (though, in fact, nearly always invisible) climax of the view from their drawing-room windows, these comely mansions are at first sight intensely alluring. Few of their owners, however, can bear to live in them for more than three or four months in the year. When the sun is not out, a distinguished dreariness envelops mansions and landscape alike; the burden of the superior past lies heavy upon these houses, which are of many periods, from the little Château de Beauregard at Serrières, with its sixteenth-century tower, to the baroque splendours of Colombier—crowned as these are by the Château de Vaudijon, a minor masterpiece of a later, Imperial epoch, adorned inside and out by the classical reliefs of David Calamé. Colombier has been, indeed, a country retreat since Roman times; with its heavy-handed castle, its First Empire Protestant Church, and the memory, august but dim, of Madame de Charrière's residence in the town, it is worth an hour in anybody's itinerary.

The southern end of Lake Neuchâtel, though strictly in the Pays de Vaud, must be considered here. It is once again great Roman ground. Orbe was once the favourite retreat of the axed Roman official; at Yverdon the sulphurous springs attracted many visitors, and the skeleton of a Roman castle has been discerned on the site of the present massive Savoyard château. There are few traces of the Romans at Orbe to-day, and fewer still of the time (in the seventh century A.D.) when the town was the capital of Transjuran-Burgundy; but at Yverdon there are many souvenirs of a later epoch. Indeed, this is one of the noblest small towns in the country, and its present state of dignified petrifaction cannot detract from the beauty of the scene or its brilliant and enlightened associations. At Yverdon were printed the explosive folios of the *Encyclopédie* of Diderot and d'Alembert; Rochet of Yverdon placed his elegant bookseller's label upon many of the best books of the period, and these may still be found in the antiquaries of Geneva and Neuchâtel. To this beneficent activity was added the long struggle of Pestalozzi to keep in being the Institute in which he sought to instruct both pupils and masters alike in new and humaner methods of education. The Château of Yverdon had never been pressed into better service; and although in the end Pestalozzi did not prevail against the forces of reaction, his twenty years at Yverdon have cast a glow of humanity over the history of the town. In the main square of Yverdon the château, built in 1260 by Peter II of Savoy, is in arresting contrast with the other public buildings, most of which date from the reigns of Louis XV and XVI. On the one side, the bulk of the four medieval towers which squat like gigantic toads at the corners of the château; their blistered, horny and deeply fissured sides confront the suave façades designed for the Protestant church, in 1757, by Jean-Michel Billon, a Genevese architect who had previously built two very accomplished houses (Grand Rue 11 and Place de la Taconnerie 10) in his native city. The third side of this curious triangle is made up by the Hôtel de Ville, erected in 1769, in which is housed a small collection of Roman remains.

All these are faded grandeurs. Most of what is positive in the canton of Neuchâtel has moved north, to La Chaux-de-Fonds. The development of this town, though very recent in date, is really a rationalization of ancient custom. For the Jura is uncomfortable country—during the winter it enjoys a climate compared by Ramuz to that of the Siberian tundras—and during these long periods of enforced leisure the Jurassian devised for himself a second occupation. He learned to excel, in fact, in the anxious craft of watchmaking. The extreme thinness and clarity of the air are favourable to his efforts, and he himself is temperamentally well equipped to master the problems of the clocksmith. At La Chaux-de-Fonds this inherited skill has been exploited on the scale of modern industry, and a town of some fifty thousand inhabitants has sprung up around the skeleton of a village rebuilt in the last decade of the eighteenth century. Like its neighbour Le Locle, La Chaux-de-Fonds is built at an altitude of 3,000 feet; it has its own aerodrome, and even its own annual carnival. Barely a dozen years old, the Braderie is held in September along the length of the rue Leopold-Robert ("Switzerland's longest street"), and is a vast combination, very Swiss in temper, of jumble sale and battle of flowers.

For the older civilization of the Jura, I need point only to the ancient roofs of Romainmôtier (28) and the delicate steeple of its abbey church. Here one may envisage the period, as remote as anything in Christian history, when the Jura was a place to which monks retired for solitude and contemplation. There has been a church at

28 Remainmôtier : the
Tour de l'Horloge (*left*)

29 Neuchâtel : the
Château (*below*)

30 The Town and the Château

31 The Hôpital de Ville (1761-5 ; *architect, Pierre-François Paris*)

PORRENTRUY

Romainmôtier since the fifth or sixth century; the present building was begun in the eleventh, and amended or expanded in the course of nearly five hundred years. In this lower part of the Jura, cattle and pinewoods are the great resource of the inhabitants; it is a country of lofty plateaux, often with high-lying lakes in their midst, where visitors may count on finding an untroubled pastoral existence. Towards the north, where the frontier lies along the line of the Doubs, we leave the canton of Neuchâtel and enter, however illogically, the canton of Berne. This is still French-speaking, French-feeling country. The beautiful town of Porrentruy (30, 31) is unrecognizable beneath its German name of Pruntrut, and the whole landscape has a largeness of mould, a liberal splendour, which belong to the Franche Comté rather than to the neat pasturage of the Bernese dairy-country. This north-west peninsula is probably the least-visited part of Switzerland. The mountainous forest-road from Délémont to Porrentruy is as fine as anything in the country, but few tourists attempt this grassy switchback, and few go tumbling down the precipitous gully which leads to St. Ursanne. Wild horses are common in this delectable region; but even they, in proverbial fashion, have failed to drag many visitors to the Jura Bernois. The error is gross, but historic. This province has rarely been given its due meed of praise. In 1815, when it was decreed at the Congress of Vienna that the area should be given over to the city of Berne in exchange for Aargau and the Vaud, the rulers of Berne were so unjust as to say that "they've taken away our good cellar and our well-stocked granary, and what have we got in their stead? A beastly attic!" But attics are sometimes the most interesting part of the house.

In 1529, when Basle went over to the Reformation, the Prince-Bishop (and what title could be more splendid?) left the city in which his predecessors had held court for nearly a thousand years, and removed to Porrentruy. Even there, the reformed religion had many partisans, and for some fifty years it looked as if the town had been dowered with untenable grandeurs; but in June 1575 a new Bishop, Jacques-Christophe Blarer, was elected, and from that day onwards Porrentruy began to be one of the small capitals of Europe. Of its monuments, the parish church dates in part from the middle of the eleventh century, and on the hill above the town the Castle can boast two medieval towers; those who climb the larger of these towers will be rewarded with a sensational view of the town, and of the Ajoie plain, on which the forests are spread like a hearth-rug. Everything else in Porrentruy dates from the era of prosperity which Blarer succeeded in bringing about. Not all his successors (he died in 1608) were as clever as he; the double duties of Bishop and Prince were not easy to sustain, and between 1730 and 1740 there was something like an attempt at revolution in the diocese. But such things have left little trace; the headsman and his block have vanished from the main street of Porrentruy, and there remain only the monuments of a beneficent reign and the scrupulous care, more Bernese than French, with which they are kept up. The Jesuit church, built at the beginning of the seventeenth century, and its contemporary, the Jesuit school, are now disaffected from the faith which built them; the castle underwent successive but always tasteful enlargements as one ruler succeeded another; the one remaining town-gate, the Porte de France, and the noble Fontaine de la Suisse, with its martial statue and hexagonal basin, both recall the new-born pride of the little capital in the 1560s; and from the other extremity of the Bishops' reign I must single out the three fine creations of Pierre-François Paris. These were all built in the 1760s, and they are now the Hôtel de Ville, the Hospital and the Post Office; few small towns can show so much good building in the service of a single idea. Since the Bishops were turned out, in 1792, Porrentruy has changed only a little; and I know of few pleasanter places in Switzerland than the silent, aerial uplands in which it lies, or the little botanical garden in which local heroes are enskied in portrait busts with corselets of ivy, and *Fraxinus Excelsior* to mark the entrance gate.

St. Ursanne (32) has never known the transitory grandeurs of a Bishop's court. Its sanctity dates from the seventh century, when St. Ursanne's hermitage became a recognized place of pilgrimage, and the present abbey church was begun in the second half of the twelfth century, under the surveillance of the Bishop of Basle. Like the town itself, it is on a small scale, but of trance-like beauty. The south door, so memorably alive to the movement of the sun, with Christ enthroned in majesty, St. Ursanne studiously upright in his niche, and a seated Virgin of singular nobility; the fourteenth-century cloister, with its pre-Raphaelite graveyard; St. Ursanne recumbent in his grotto with a bear to keep watch by his side; the shadowy phantoms of late Gothic frescoes in the chapels on the south side of the nave—all these are things of wonder. The little church sits in the encircling town like a walnut in its shell; the curve of the Doubs seals off the town from the sharply rising uplands to the south; to west and east, the gates, strong and narrow, of the seventeenth century still stand to control all traffic. Hardly a house has altered for two hundred years; on the narrow bridge over the Doubs, St. Nepomucène stands with all the assurance of the baroque style of 1728 (33). Gourmets may be assured, moreover, that nowhere in Switzerland does one eat better than at St. Ursanne.

32 The Bridge Tower (1522) and the Bridge (*left*)

33 Statue of St. Nepomucène (1728) on the Bridge (*right*)

ST. URSANNE

34 Morat : the fifteenth-century fortifications

After visiting these two towns one must either go forward into France, and so out of this book, or back into the rich centre of the canton of Berne. To do this, it is convenient to pass by Biel, and to make a detour into the canton of Fribourg. I do not know these cantons as well as I should wish. It is difficult to get to know them in a short time; outside their cities and large towns, they are not organized for tourism, and the stray visitor knows himself to be superfluous as he bowls along the dusky roads, overhangs the gorge in which a putty-coloured river moves quietly towards the distant sea, or lies in the rolling prairies round Schwarzenburg and catches the waxen apple as it drops from the bough. It is mostly quiet country. The gentlest of rivers and canals (the Thièle at Yverdon, the Broye at Payerne) replace the tomboyish abandon of the mountain stream. It is country, too, in which French shades off into German in the space of a hundred yards, and where it is possible to find, as at Neuveville, a small town in which, though it is architecturally of pure German extraction, one hears only the pellucid French of the Neuchâtelois. It is country in which lake and marsh are sometimes confused, as at Morat; and in which, as at the Château d'Oron, an exterior can betoken only a medieval fortress of the most uninhibited sort, while within there are the *boiseries* of the eighteenth century, a Gothic-ceilinged library ranging from the Pléïade to Beaumarchais, and a salon in which fox and hare are hunted upon a painted frieze. It is not industrial country; and in a town such as Biel, which has grown fourfold in the last hundred years, the office and factory quarter has not been allowed to encroach upon the old town. Biel is largely bi-lingual, but in its sixteenth-century quarter (the Burggasse, for instance, and the Ringplatz) it is so intensely old German in feeling as to be almost a burlesque of the neat and shining towns which attracted, before 1939, so many simple-minded visitors. Those who enjoy such ambiguities will savour the double provenance of such a town as Morat (27, 34).

Morat lies above its own reedy, bird-haunted lake. It is a walled town, with fifteenth-century fortifications still intact, and famous for the battle of 1476, in which Charles the Bold and his Burgundian army were soundly beaten by the Swiss. There is much to see at Morat, but the visitor from the Vaud will be curious to detect the first signs of Germanic influence. These are many—the sudden, fastidious elegance of the sign "Apotheke" beneath the arcades; the far-overhanging eaves, each as deeply hollowed as the hull of a ketch; and above all the triumphant Bernese Gate, with its narrow entrance overweighted by a clock- and bell-tower of metropolitan proportions. Thus far does Berne assert its power.

While at Morat, it would be foolish to miss the opportunity of visiting Avenches. Whereas many of the principal Roman settlements in Switzerland have been overlaid by later building and can be glimpsed only by a flight of the imagination, Avenches, or Aventicum, lies in open country; and the whole vast *enceinte*, which forms a polygon with a circumference of over four miles, can be tramped round, if not seen, in perfect freedom. It lies in marsh country, near where the Canal de la Broye meanders invisibly towards the lake; only after a few miles do the shallow hills of the Vully arise hesitantly from the flat. The theatre, the amphitheatre, the standing pilaster of the Cigognier, the vomitorium, the other more vestigial relics of Roman building, and the medals, bronzes, mosaics, keys, pipes, pens, pins and other trophies in the museum—all compose an arresting ensemble, from which, however, the finest item has rather unfairly been removed to a grander museum. This is, of course, the bust in pure gold of a Roman emperor of the Antonine period, which was discovered at Avenches as recently as 1939. One cannot be brought so close to the Antonine age without experiencing a moment of vivid emotion—for it was then, in the view of such good judges as Gibbon and Renan, that the harmonious state was finally created, and thenceforward that the world began, once and for all, to go wrong. As Montesquieu says of Antoninus Pius: "Merely to speak of this emperor creates within oneself a secret pleasure; and one cannot read of his life without experiencing the tenderest of emotions; such is its effect that, in thinking better of mankind, one also thinks better of oneself." For those who, like myself, support the ideal of decentralized museums, there is something exasperating in the removal of this bust from Avenches.

It is said that material from Aventicum was used in building the abbey church of Payerne (37). Whether true or not, this could hardly enhance the wonder with which we must regard this vast edifice, so surprising an addition to the slumbering valley of the Broye. Long disaffected from the Church, it served until very recently as a garrison, fire-station, lock-up and granary. This procedure has at least given us the opportunity to study a Romanesque interior of absolutely first-class quality without any of the distracting furniture of assent which normally obscures the creation of the original builders. The limestone, alternately pink and yellow, has matured to a texture of quite bewildering beauty, and nothing could exceed the awe with which we tread beneath the great barrel-vaulted roof. Most noble, too, is the stern of the church, with its clustering apses and fragmentary wall-paintings. The tower and spire are of the fifteenth and seventeenth centuries respectively. It is near Payerne, in the forest of

Boulex and the valley of the Broye, that the traveller's will is taxed to the utmost: with a bottle of St. Saphorin in one's bag, and some sandwiches of Payerne ham, it is more tempting to ride through the sun-bright *allées* of the forest, or to drift with oars relaxed on the serpentine stream of the Broye, than to drive in a cloud of white dust towards the flowered fountains of Berne. Some of my own ignorance must be ascribed to this cause; not all detours are fruitful, but there is one which I must enjoin to all readers—to Fribourg, and thence down the Sarine valley to Gruyères.

Fribourg, like Berne, is built on the bend of a river; but where Berne is symmetrical and its terrain flat and regular, Fribourg has profited by the extreme irregularities of its site to compose a sequence of giddying perspectives (35). Now above, now below, the visitor is presented with street after street of late Gothic dwellings, sometimes so carefully preserved as to suggest a royal doll's house, and sometimes as deliquescent as an aged Brie. There is something for every taste in Fribourg—in the Eglise des Cordeliers, an altar-piece by the Master of the Carnation; step-roofed barracks of the early nineteenth century, with striped shutters, in the Quartier de la Planche; the ancient gates and turreted fortifications of the city, many of them dating from the 1380s; and the new University to speak, not always happily, for our own generation. Since the six-teenth century Fribourg has been a great Catholic centre; the tra-dition is still maintained in the firmly Maritainist atmosphere of the University, but it is from the original migration, four centuries ago, that the city takes most of its colour. No fewer than eight of the superb fountains of Fribourg were erected in the sixteenth century; the covered wooden Pont de Berne is dated 1580, the Prefecture 1586, the Hôtel de Ville 1500–22; and I can only regret that the Jordil family from Geneva should have been so over-zealous as to complete the Cathedral tower, Fribourg's most conspicuous monument, eight years before the end of the fifteenth century. Yet individual buildings do not greatly alter the general impression of Fribourg, which is that of a sixteenth-century hill-town, of whose most ravishing perspectives many are held together by the slender but commanding statues of the three fine sculptors, Hans Geiler, Hans Gieng and Stephan Ammann, who dignified the city with nine of its most beautiful fountains. In the seventeenth century Fribourg produced an interesting church-architect in Hans Franz Reyff. Originally employed on the fortifications between the Porte de Morat and the river-bank, he built between 1647 and 1650 the Lorettokapelle, which lies above the town on the heights which face the Pont de St. Jean and the Pont du Milieu. It is worth the

climb; and this can be arranged to display equally the two tremendous suspension bridges by which the Sarine was spanned in the
adventurous 1830s. The little chapel lies like a scale model above the
wooded slopes, its rusticated elegance enhanced by the lifesize
statues which confine themselves, with some difficulty, to the narrow
niches which Reyff has devised for them. Three years after com-
pleting this chapel, Reyff began simultaneously on two new commissions—the churches of the Ursulinerinnenkloster, in the rue
de Lausanne, and the Visitanterinnenkloster, in the rue de Morat.
Only a ground-plan can convey the originality of the latter design, in
which the square nave, flanked on three of its sides by more than
semi-circular bays, and on the fourth by a semi-circular entrance-
hall, is lit from above by a large octagonal tambour. Fribourg is so
full of good medieval churches that it may seem perverse to dwell
instead upon this original but minor artist; but at the cost of straying
yet farther from my appointed path, I shall pause for a moment to
discuss the question of food in Switzerland. English visitors often
speak as if Switzerland were a good country in which to eat. This is
a great error. The materials of Swiss meals are almost always excellent, and there is nowhere in Switzerland in which, given normal
ingenuity, it is not possible to gorge. But Swiss cooking will not often
satisfy a fastidious taste; and the larger the town, the more hazardous
the adventure. Though tempted, in human charity, to strew warn-
ings and invitations along the whole length of my narrative, I have
long decided that, in general, it would be invidious to pick on
individual restaurants for praise or blame. The purpose, then, of this
lengthy exordium? To break my own rule and single out two places
in which one eats as well as in a French restaurant of good class: the
Hôtel Bleu at St. Ursanne, and the Restaurant de la Couronne at
Fribourg. There may be others as good, but I have not yet found
them. They are blessedly free, moreover, from the defects of Swiss
service. At its best, this has a charming spontaneity; at its worst, it
combines the humour of the stoat with the grave pageantry of the
tortoise. In the restaurants I have named, it is found at its best.

One could continue in this gastronomic vein by remarking that
the Gruyère region, with its honey, cheese and river trout, is one of
the best eating-grounds in the country. Bulle, Montbovon, Grand-
villard are robust country towns in the radiant valley of the Sarine.
Peaks there are in plenty—but not so high as to obtrude upon the
life of the pasturage below; it is there that one may hope to hear the
Ranz des Vaches, beloved of Berlioz, as the cowman rallies his
majestic beasts. Gruyères itself is built upon a little eminence above
the valley. It owes its importance to the rôle played, in the sixteenth

35   Fribourg : the Lower Town

37 Payerne : the Romanesque Nave
of the Abbey Church

36 Arlesheim : the Abbey Church, with stucco work
of 1760 by J. A. Feuchtmayr

century, by the Comtes de Gruyère in the affairs of the canton of Fribourg. One would be a sad curmudgeon not to find it pretty, as one walks up between the decorated house-fronts of 1560 and 1570 to where the castle sits waiting for the wheel of pomp and circumstance to turn full circle. In the courtyard, with its covered galleries, plays were once given, and tournaments; but nothing is heard there to-day but the fresh wind from the Oberland, and the most original feature of the castle is the salon in which the panels were painted by Corot, Barthelemy Menn and Fr.-Louis Français. Poor Français! The comparison is unfair to his *dessus-de-portes*, which show at least a certain anatomical ingenuity. Both Corot and Menn were in capital form; and in Corot's panels one may see motifs from the valley below, transmuted and etherealized by this most seraphic of painters.

*   *   *   *   *

One can motor great distances in Switzerland and hardly ever be out of sight of a timber-mill. Wood is, in fact, the great building material of Switzerland. It burns easily, of course, and there are few villages in the country which have not, somewhere in their history, the memory of a disastrous fire. But it is also easily replaced, and it makes up in a style which never grows ridiculous or out of date. This is why an ugly village, with obsolete and loathly survivals of some ill-judged venture of the past, is rare in Switzerland. In some areas the use of wood results in buildings of fantastic complexity, in which wood has been persuaded to seem as plastic as stucco, or to bear lengthy inscriptions engraved with the art of a fine calligrapher. This is nowhere more evident than in the canton of Berne—in the Emmental (5) or the Gürbetal. The wide verandas of these houses, and the eaves which reach almost to the ground, betoken a life led between the extremes of winter, when the snow may be several feet thick and patterned with the prints of rabbit and hare, and summer, when the whole house will dry out like an old mackintosh beneath a broiling sun. These are ark-like dwellings, whose style has not changed for many generations. How must the city of Berne appear to those who stick out the winter in the upper Emmental? One can be sure that to them it must be a place of unequivocal magic. Simply to see the trams leap through their grassy enclosure in the Bubenbergplatz, or to wander in the Waisenhausplatz on market day when it is piled with fruit and flowers like a masque of Ceres, or on a wet afternoon to amble in comfort through the arcades of the Kramgasse —these are pleasures even for us; but we are not really adapted to Berne. This is a city of childlike enchantment, in which it does not do to find the bears too fat, or the cinemas too early, or the interior

65

of the Münster too late. Innocence is the key to Berne. A sceptical eye is out of place, as the gold and scarlet fountains rise from their nests of geraniums, and the enormous clocks clang out the hour. These arcades, these fountains, these bears have existed in one form or another for five centuries. They are permanent features of Berne and the elaborate pantomime of noon at the Clock Tower on the Kramgasse (when bears count the hour, a cock crows and the Duke of Zähringen strikes the hour) is also attuned rather to the faculty of wonder than to rational analysis. The Münster St. Vinzenz at Berne (38) is the latest in date of all Swiss cathedrals. Only in 1440 was Matthäus Ensinger, who had assisted his father with the cathedrals of Ulm and Strasburg, entrusted with the plans for the new building. He, his son and his grandson were all concerned with the Berne Münster between 1440 and 1483, and at the end of the century Erhart Küng built the two rectangular storeys of the tower (which was not finally completed till 1893) and also the Last Judgment over the west door, a composition which must really be deciphered rather than examined. Early in the sixteenth century the choir was given its present elaborate lierne vaulting; Niklaus Manuel, best of Bernese artists, is said to have painted the many-coloured bosses for this vaulting, and also to have supervised the carving of the choir-stalls. The Münster fits admirably into the line of the city as it lies, surrounded on three sides by the Aar, and dominated by the wooded uplands of the Mittelland; but it is a less distinguished building than the Heiliggeistkirche, built in 1726–9 by Nikolaus Schildknecht. This architect, like Stürler, who built the Erlacherhof, 47 Junkerngasse, was not given any other great chances in Berne; elsewhere, indeed, the individual building merges into the general festivity of the city, and it is for us to merge with it—discarding for the moment our natural coolness of judgment, and seeking to recapture, in the Schänzli or the quieter beer-gardens by the Aar, the atmosphere most appropriate to Berne: that of the *Kermesse*, the genial, bearlike abandon of the untormented, which caused an earlier traveller to remark, of Bernese waltz-parties, that "the life and spirit of their dances fill a foreigner with astonishment and can scarcely be conceived by those who have never seen them".

38 Berne: the Münster rising above the Herrengasse

39   The Matterhorn and the Riffelsee

III

The Valais

The Rhône Valley—Sierre—Sion—The Lotschental—Brigue

FOR many visitors to Lac Léman, the valley of the Rhône has
the aspect of a dusty and unvisited *arrière-boutique*. Tourism
stops at Chillon; and even on the finest day, when the spectacular escarpments of the Meillerie stand out in deep, blue-shadowed
relief, the estuary of the Rhône often glowers in what is called (in
an indispensable French idiom) "covered weather". The Rhône delta
is perfectly flat. Ideal for toxophily or the testing of a theodolite, it is
not very inviting for ordinary visitors; and these habitually dart off
to the right, up to Champéry, or to the left, up to Villars and Leysin.
Only in these elevated resorts does the apparatus of tourism recur;
the traveller nosing his way up the motor-road will find, from
2,500 feet onwards, the words TEA-ROOM and, less plausibly,
JARDIN ANGLAIS, in comforting profusion. The flat ground at the
bottom is not exciting, but a fine writer can turn it into a private
Arcadia; Ramuz has done so in his *Vendanges*. Ourselves lose heart
as the steamboats and the black-headed gulls of the Léman give
place to the damp and spongy terrain of the delta, but Ramuz, faithful to the images of his childhood, reveals these desolate brakes as a
land full of enchantment. Sprigs of elder, he tells us, provided
excellent squirts; dragon-fly and salamander made every pool a place
of wonder; more sinister creatures, flies of blue velvet and the toad
with its folds of skin, appealed equally to these little boys, for whom
the scent of a toadstool trodden underfoot was intensely alluring.
The ground, always soft and porous, often gave way altogether; and
in these places pools of water, at once clear and perfectly black,
would form, or the roots of trees, "which elsewhere were hidden,
here showed their whitish tufts like the hair of a dead woman whose
corpse is floating head downwards".

The Valais is a country of extremes, and the traveller who has
admired such feats of engineering as the Grimsel reservoir and the
new Susten Pass may be surprised to find that in the upper regions
of the Valais whole villages may depend for their water, in summer,
upon a system of primitive troughs or wooden pipes; these *bisses* are
fed from a stream which rises high up, at glacier level. The glacier
itself may look white and silky from the floor of the valley, but if one

ventures near, it reveals itself as possessing the colour of an army blanket and the texture of the tongue (ridged, slimy and scaly) of some prehistoric monster. Not for nothing did Tennyson say of one glacier that "it looks as if a thousand London seasons had passed over it". Prodigies of skill and endurance must be lavished in the Valais upon the simplest achievements of husbandry. Barley and rye must be persuaded to grow at 6,000 feet; grain has only between four and six months to ripen; black earth must be strewn upon the snow to make it melt, and the grain, when cut, is spread upon wooden stands in order to dry and complete its ripening. Most holdings in the Valais are small; more than half of them are of less than twelve acres. The passionate and densely goitred peasantry of this area are among the least attractive of Swiss peoples, but the landscape and some of its monuments have a more personal and a less obvious hold upon the observer than those of many more famous cantons. Sion (40) is beyond question the most original town in Switzerland; and east of Sion the cicada begins. The Valais is not so much Mediterranean as Iberian in tone. There is intensive, though inconclusive, political feeling in the Valais; an acceptance, elsewhere unknown in Switzerland, of violence and cruelty; and a positive, healthy indifference to the foreign visitor. The Valais is self-sufficing, incurious country; it is as if it carried within itself enough extremes to satisfy a lifetime of wonderment. Another page of Ramuz recalls how sharply this country reverts from the fertile asparagus-bearing plain to the topmost, polar landscape above Arolla. "A few hours' walk", he remarks, "and it is as if one had travelled thousands of miles northwards." Many villages in the Valais aggravate the oddities of their situation by transferring themselves bodily, according to the season, up and down from the valley to the heights. The homes of the Valaisans, like their climates and their means of livelihood, exist in layers, one on top of the other. Part of the year is spent among the vines, part in the village itself, half-way up the Val d'Hérens or the Val d'Anniviers, and part among the high pastures. With the alternation of these three lodgments a man can make enough to support himself, his family and his beasts. On the outskirts of many villages one may still see a primitive mill, with its moss-grown wheel; with this, and the force of a mountain stream, flour was made from grain reaped among the *mayens* at the top of the valley. The older men can still show suits of a rich brown wool, woven from the fleece of their sheep, and shoes made in the village from the leather of their beasts. The seasonal migrations still go on—up and down, 3,000 feet at a time; often a whole village will march together, with fifes and drums to encourage them through the rough tunnels, along the side of the

40   Sion : the twin hills of Tourbillon and Valère

41   Brigue : the Stockalper Palace (1641-7)

42   Sion : from the Château of Tourbillon

gorges and up the steep and dusty tracks beside which water runs, white and smoky, in its *bisse*. And mules go with them, each with its laden panniers of wood or leather. Level ground is rare in the Valais once the Rhône has been left below. The extreme dryness (Sion has the lowest rainfall in Switzerland) also has its problems.

The Valais is wonderful country for the visitor. Mr. Cyril Connolly has admirably described "the burnt-up white landscape of little African hills, like the homes of Spanish troglodytes, the rainless apricot country between Sion and Sierre. Here the cicada is found, and up each long lateral valley is some curiosity of wildness; women of Saracen descent, smugglers' headquarters, rare Arolla pines, or the archaic village-kingdom, with strange costumes and marriage-laws, of Evolène." For the visitor all this is just another batch of sensations, perhaps rather more vivid than most—remote, certainly, from the hygienic precision of German Switzerland, and remote also from the languors of the Ticino. Urban persons can only guess at the rewards of life in the Valais. Do the satisfactions and the silent felicities lie waiting, like soldanella beneath February snows, for those who can stay behind to greet them? Ramuz would have it so. A London Sunday (even, one might say, a Kinsington Sunday) has little to put beside the approved Saturnalia of a Sunday in the Valais. All nature conspires, it would seem, to heighten the Biblical gaieties of the seventh day.

Very early, even at dawn, when the summits around us are first touched with rose and themselves burst into flower as if they wanted to be the first to take part in the festivities, the carillon begins to thread its notes upon the needle-point of the steeple. Sunday clothes are brought out. The men are newly shaven, rejuvenated, with a week's growth of beard cut away; the girls have washed with cold water and rubbed their cheeks to make them red; everything is clean and new. Everybody makes himself beautiful, the men with white shirts, the girls with thin Sunday hats trimmed with black and blue velvet, a jacket of alpaca with silvered lapels, and silk kerchiefs knotted in front and flung broadly around their shoulders. Before every house the sun has laid a great bar of shade, like a second threshold. "They still have festivals in the Valais," Ramuz goes on, "and real festivals—by which I mean occasions for rejoicing in common; that is to say, that they still live as a community (that is what makes up for the hardness of their lives). Along the length of the village street they plant branches of acacia which have been cut in the neighbouring forest; it is the moment at which they are in flower; they flower in pink and in white all along the street until the village no longer knows itself in its new dress. Between these two blossoming hedges the procession comes, and it is a wonderful one. The whole village takes part. A fanfare of trumpeting soldiers. The soldiers of to-day with their rifles and steel helmets—for when they return from military service they bring their equipment with them. Old uniforms: some from the days when Swiss soldiers served abroad; uniforms from the armies of Naples, of France and of Rome; tall shakos with a scarlet plume, enormous epaulettes, tunics with breastplate, baldrics of white leather, laid crosswise on the breast, tight breeches, top boots and gaiters. After the dull, earthern colours which the modern army has adopted in the hope of making itself invisible, come these dazzling inventions, chosen with the contrary object of being seen from afar. Next, the dais, where the priest is holding our Saviour in his two hands; then the daughters of the village, in their white veils; and then everyone, everyone who can stand up on his legs: the oldest bent double, with a stick to prevent them falling over forwards; the infirm, with their crutches; women who hold close against them the packet of pink wool in which reposes their newest-born; everyone, because here there is still unanimity."

This great poet of Valaisian life has a page for every season, but it is to the vines that, like the men of the Valais themselves, he gives his best energies. The vines of the Valais (43) have not as a rule the spectacular neatness of those along the Léman—the terraces lodged, against nature and against reason, on the rocky slopes of the Côte de Lavaux; the blue flowers, tufted in the yellow surface of the support-ing walls; and, as one looks down from the corniche road in spring, the yellow forestry of the canes. In the Valais there are vines on the flat bottom of the valley, and others niched low on those parallel ranges of which the topmost reaches are cooked and re-cooked by the sun to the colours, all blue and scarlet, of the hinderparts of a blue mandril in the zoo. In the Valais, vines are planted literally into the rock, at any point where a pocket or cup has allowed the intrusion of even a very little earth. It is lizard and grasshopper country, traversed only by mule-tracks and uncompanionable paths. A little higher, there may be another of those layers which compose the Valaisian landscape. The earth is flinty in these parts; brambles and schist separate the tiny plots of vine. Suddenly a little Eden will come into view—peach, pear and apple-trees based in luxuriant grass; and nearby some rude houses of white stone, staging points in the seasonal journey from mountain to plain. The village itself may be a thousand feet or more above, accessible only by woodland paths; a low cloud may envelop us as we climb; the dust on our clothes will be like the finest sand.

Above the village, beyond the first mountain pools, through the boskage of larch and fir, are yet other houses—huts of brown wood, sheltering a kitchen, sometimes a hay-loft, sometimes also a living-room. These are the *mayens*; and here, according to Ramuz, forbidden dances are held, and the wheezing and squeaking of forbidden instruments is heard at a safe distance from the parsonical ear. Higher still, and bilberries and wild raspberries grow freely, to reward a panting traveller. Another half an hour and the rock begins to come through the moss, like an elbow through an old coat. Soon, isolated Arolla pines are the only remaining trees. Then is reached, at 6,000 feet or above, the mysterious aerial plateau, from which the snow recedes between June and September to reveal nothing but yellowy grass, odd boulders and the topmost relay of outlying houses. Ramuz describes the life led there during two months of every year—a life Theocritean, even Abrahamic, in its plainness and regularity, a life such as one imagines must be led in the mountains of Tibet. The daily provision of butter, signed each morning with the mark of the Cross; a store of cheese, enlarged every day in readiness for the winter months; the erections of stone and slate, hardly to be called houses, in which beasts and owners shelter at night; the coffin-like beds slung from the wall, with at most a little straw at the bottom; dwellings such as Lear and his Fool were glad to find; homes stiff with the smell of smoke, wet clothes and the grease of sheep's wool. Superior persons will be surprised to find, however, that the spoons, ladles, churns, buckets, troughs and tubs of this primitive community are designed and decorated with a beauty and assurance to which no manufacturer could now lay claim.

This upland colony breaks camp after eight or nine weeks, and the whole enterprise, with its animals, provisions, implements and stocks of butter and cheese, moves down to the village. Above the plateau which they have left there is nothing but the glacier; nothing but the space and silence of pre-history.

*   *   *   *   *

For those, like myself, whose thoughts revert constantly, though in no envious sense, to the Elysian Fields, there is one scene upon which it is particularly agreeable to dwell: the moment at which, while the poets sit gossiping among meadows thick with asphodel, their women friends bicker quietly in an adjoining glade. Miss Brawne and Miss Siddal might come to terms; but among the foreigners (for thus they must be considered, even in this supra-national society) differences will not be so easily composed. The friends of Rilke may give trouble to an exceptional degree; bee-like in his inconstancy, though buzzing mainly among the more rarefied blooms of our European garden, Rilke could boast a company of friends whose names witness not only to an unusual delicacy of choice but also to that pathology of nomenclature which often afflicts an overblown society. From most of them he demanded the qualities of a kindly baggage-animal, combined with the greatest possible amplitude of means and station. Their names read like a directory of vanished European life, and one cannot suppose that he was indifferent to the Straussian orchestration of such conjunctions as von der Mühll-Burckhardt, Wunderly-Volkart, Schmidt-Paulli, Thurn and Taxis Hohenlohé, Schenk-Schweinsberg, Burckhardt-Schatzmann, Andreas-Salome, zu Solms-Lauback and von Nordeck zu Rabenau. Some of them (Ouckama-Knoop, for example) display a Pan-like invention in their search for new combinations of sound; to others there still adheres an ancient tradition of simple grandeur. Nearly all these ladies were concerned, in the summer and autumn of 1919, to equip their hero with a luxurious retreat in which he could recover from the war. Enervated by a short period of nominal military service, and the prey of personal defeatism in its most grandiose form, he was offered a range of eyries such as few poets have been so fortunate as to glimpse. The possibilities of Venice, Padua, Leipzig and Schloss Lautschin were weighed against memories of Duino, Meudon, Anacapri and Borgeby-gard. An ideal loneliness was Rilke's preferred state: a tower-bound, dispeopled existence in surroundings such as those enjoyed by Villiers' Count Axel of Auersburg, or by the Hamlet of Laforgue when he gazed out through leaded windows upon that farthest corner of a great park in which are gathered "the débris of the green-house and the moribund bouquets of ephemeral galas". Life catches up with art in the end, and when Rilke at last hit upon the tower which he needed, it was in Switzerland—a mile or two, in fact, from the point which we have now reached.

Rilke was, if anything, disposed not to settle in Switzerland. He shared the conventional distaste of sensitive persons for Alpine landscape; the horrors of this seemed to him to have been aggravated, if not indeed actually brought on, by the admiration of nineteenth-century travellers. Irony was his best defence; that, and the habit of drawing the blinds of his first-class compartment, had preserved him in more comfortable times. Now Switzerland had become, as so often since, the only enclave of normal European life, and Rilke paid visits of varying length to friends at Nyon, Soglio, Ascona, Locarno and Schloss Schönenberg near Basle. He was not an easy guest. Royal privileges, no less, were demanded; and since Rilke, though

43   Vineyards in the Valais

44, 45 Fête-Dieu Celebrations in the Valais

not often loving, was very often loved,[1] they were often accorded. Castle Berg, a seventeenth-century castle on the Irchel, proved more acceptable than other houses whose owners either had not given Rilke the best rooms or had shown an intolerable tendency to remain in residence themselves during the period of his visit. But in January 1921 he left Berg, and negotiations were reopened in Bohemia, Carinthia and the Euganean Hills. His "ten minimum requirements" were hard to satisfy: attendance at Basler spiritualist séances proved of no value, and it can only have been by chance that in a hairdresser's window in Sierre there was discovered a photograph of the house in which he was to experience a creative period more intense than almost any in the annals of poetry.

The Château de Muzot is a very plain and rather dullish building in a style quite common in the Valais. (The thirteenth-century Majorie at Sion is very similar to it.) Contemporary photographs show that in 1921 it had the air of a castellated hutch. It is perhaps two kilometres from Sierre, and lies in orchard country, a little way from the road to Montana. In summer an Arcadian landscape surrounds the little house. Apples and quinces, bored with life on the bough, fall harmlessly among long grass. Little streams run noisily in search of level ground. The vine-arbours of the house itself are empurpled by the magnificent grapes of the neighbourhood. Few people pass, though binoculars will often reveal a shirt-sleeved poet in the shelving ground towards Sion. Beyond Sierre, the view extends up the narrow Val d'Anniviers to the discreet fastness of the Weisshorn. Up at Montana, behind the house, wealthy persons plod round the golf-course in the hope of making the day seem shorter, but at Muzot there is nothing to tempt one to exertion. The house is now furnished in a style of cosmopolitan luxury very appropriate to the most famous of its tenants; and though the fruits of the earth are agreeably present, the labour which produces them does not obtrude. On such a day it is tempting to question the impressions of Paul Valéry, who visited Rilke at Muzot at Easter 1924. Rilke at that time had just spent three months almost completely alone. The house, standing by itself in a forbidding landscape of rock and snow, appeared to Valéry the image of solitude and of (as he put it) an excessive intimacy with silence. The interior, ill-lit and cumbered with gloomy old furniture, struck a natural chill into Valéry's heart. To Ramuz, staunchest of local patriots, the little watch-tower was quite congenial. Its walls (a yard thick) were heated like a stove by the rough sunshine of the Valais, and in his lumber-bedroom

[1] A phrase which, together with much else, I have borrowed from Dr. E. M. Butler's admirable *Rilke*, Cambridge University Press (1941).

on the second floor he was pleasantly baked. So avid a collector of Swiss sensations could not but welcome the apparition after nightfall of several scores of homing bats; and as they filed through the narrow tunnel of his window and quietly clung by their feet to the ceiling, Ramuz gave out (we have his word for it) a sigh of pleasure.

Rilke himself took an unbounded delight in the amenities of the castle and its chivalrous associations. Its old stones, grey and violet in winter, were so gilded and embrowned in summer that they seemed to Rilke like the walls of Andalusia. Within, the woodwork, coffers and fenestration reverted to the dreamland of the sixteenth century, and on one of the beams were engraved the figures MDCXVII. "Charm" would be the wrong word for the affinity which bound Rilke to Muzot; its spell had a graver aspect, and he himself spoke of the "obsessional anguish" provoked by the dark little house. The gloomy cells of Muzot became the oratories of his art, and in the shelter ("at once peasant-like and seignorial", as he once remarked) of this fortified tower he experienced, between February 2nd and 20th, 1922, the fabulous period of poetical effort in which he composed the fifty-five *Sonnets to Orpheus* and completed the ten *Duino Elegies*. The unbending landscape of the Valais, in which he had detected both Spanish and Provençal elements, thus furnished this curious little person (the image, with his spats and high collar, of a Viennese dandy) with the occasion of an outburst of music which can hardly have been exceeded since Orpheus first strung his lute.

Sierre is not a show-place. Most travellers see it only as the junction for the cosmopolitan pleasures of Montana or the simpler and rarer enjoyments of the Val d'Anniviers. Only in 1877 did a garlanded locomotive replace the diligence which until then had plied between Sierre and Brigue. The Swiss railway systems, delayed in every case by difficulties and intrigues of abnormal complexity, were especially slow to penetrate the Rhône valley; this area, indeed, had only recently been the scene of disputes and violences whose print has endured for a century. The Valais is passionate country, but its passions are not those of the surface, and a more obvious trait has become, however unfairly, the national badge of the area. Saint-Loup, to whom Proust gave every possible distinguishing mark of sophisticated elegance, could think of few replies more final than: "I suppose you take me for a cretin from the Valais?" This custom endures, but there are more positive qualities in the Valais, and Sierre has its share of them. The surrounding landscape has an aptly tumultuous history. Geology itself had set a brisk pace when

Mount Carbaccio collapsed and fell into the Rhône; "and one would aver," remarks a Swiss historian, "that Nature has not yet recovered from her surprise". Such events are rare in our own time, when even the machinery of war has generally failed to modify the physical outline of landscape; surface diversions alone occur. But at Sierre a virgin forest quickly sprang up upon the débris of the mountain, and the impatient Rhône forced its way across the field of rubbish until it had shaped for itself those diminutive canyons which one may still remark. There resulted from this what the same commentator has called "an archipelago of knolls", stretching downstream from Sierre, of which the largest, the Géronde, still shelters within itself two tiny blue lakes; sensitive local observers have likened these to "the two eyes of a child, between eyelids of golden reed". Sierre itself still carries the mark of this upheaval; for though the town is built on firm enough ground, and the original settlement has powdered away beneath the broom and the pulsatilla, certain quarters still bear the names of The Marsh and The Gravel-Pit. To-day the hills of the Vieux-Sierre have been stripped of their trees, and an aluminium works whitens the Rhône; a meridional sun (so justly included in the blazon of Sierre) coaxes a bloom upon the matchless fruit of this Noble Contrée—the apple and the apricot, the mirabelle and the golden grape. Ceres could live here, and Iris could point to

> *Thy banks with pioned and twilled brims,*
> *Which spongy April at thy hest betrims,*
> *To make cold nymphs chaste crowns; and thy broom-groves,*
> *Whose shadow the dismissed bachelor loves,*
> *Being lass-lorn; thy pole-clipt vineyard;*
> *And thy sea-marge, sterile and rocky-hard,*
> *Where thou thyself dost air.*

It is always rash for a traveller to pronounce upon the private habits of the natives. Did not Bishop Burnet, as Mr. Lunn has recently reminded us, assert in 1685 that the women of Berne "did not know what Amours were"? Allowing, therefore, the dismissed bachelor to repair to the broom-grove, and there to staunch his unwitnessed tears, we may remark a feature of the scene which Shakespeare could not have pictured to himself—the brilliant and waterless air of the Valais, so astonishing to an English eye.

From the Géronde one may glimpse, in this vivifying element, the whole town of Sierre. The Ligures, that curious race of rock-animals, and the far-ranging Celts have left little to show for their passage. Romans, Burgundians, Franks, Lombards and Saracens may also for the moment be discounted. Sierre was for a long time, however, the property of the Abbey of St. Maurice, and it is to this period that the most conspicuous building, the Château des Vidames, may be traced. (Until 1695 the Rhône followed in many parts a course different from its present one; this determined the sites of many important buildings and gave to certain areas an importance now withdrawn from them.) Most of the oldest strong-points in Sierre were destroyed either in the struggle against Amédée VII of Savoy, in 1387, or in the war against the Upper Valais in 1417. One of few exceptions to this rule is the Tour de Goubing, inside whose featureless walls may be seen the portrait of that redoubtable Antiope, the last of the Plateas; a manly sexagenarian, with fixed frown and unyielding corsage, she has been seen by philosophical writers as the symbol of that desipience of a great race which leads to an exchange of qualities between the sexes; but simpler tourists will often have encountered the double of this ancient Platea at the reception-desk of hotels. Her traditional nickname of "Joyous Beard" one must ascribe to some quirk of Valaisian humour.

The Château des Vidames was acquired in the eighteenth century by the family of de Courten at a time when they were embellishing the town with some of its splendid ornaments. Fiery and professional in the discharge of their duties, they carried arms in Flanders, the Low Countries, Catalonia, Sicily, Majorca and Languedoc. They fought for Louis XIV; they were decimated in traditional style at Fontenoy. One of them, Comte Maurice de Courten, was employed by Louis XV as Ambassador in Berlin and Vienna, and Voltaire went so far as to say that

> *Au courtisan le plus rusé,*
> *Au Gascon le plus avisé,*
> *Courten peut servir de modèle.*

Other Kings of France found faithful servants in Sierre. Louis XIII, for example, often commended Angelin de Preux, Grand-Chatelain de Sierre, for his services in the war against Spain; and another de Preux was made General of the French Empire and Governor of Seville and Toledo, only to die in 1813, a captive in "foggy and distant" England. Nor were the soldiers of God less remarkable. In his short monograph on Sierre, M. Paul de Chastonay recalls the case of Ignace de Lovina de Sierre, tutor to Archduke Charles of Austria in the last years of the seventeenth century, and eventually Bishop of Neustadt, near Vienna. The brother of this prelate became a Jesuit, and filled important diplomatic functions in Constantinople and Venice. While it would be the basest flattery to suggest that the spirit of these energetic and globe-trotting forbears can still be detected in Sierre, some of its houses at any rate retain a trace or two of the civilization which their first owners had served. How else could one account for the presence in this remote township of the elaborate Louis XIII panelling in the Château de Villa or the ceiling in the Château de Cour, with its allegorical references to the providential failure of the Fronde, or the Hôtel Pancrace de Courten, whose assumption of a full Mansardian style is relieved only by the use of *tufa* by a local artisan? The Maison Eugène de Courten offers perhaps the most delicate tribute to the civilization of France. The Swiss might be tough and assiduous soldiers (Saint-Simon remarks, for instance, their exemplary valour at Oudenarde), but they were not mere belliferous animals; and the saloon in this large and handsome house is decorated with scenes from the plays of Molière. Dalliances and embarkations offer, as always, the best opportunities to decorative painters; and as Molière is not very strong on embarkations, these are to be found in the nearby drawing-room of Pancrace de Courten.

*   *   *   *   *

The Valais needs to be interpreted by a poet, rather than by a topographer. Other parts of Switzerland have not the same quality of reserve, and it is notable that poetry about the Alps no longer leans very much upon the physical aspect of the scene. Romantic poetry about Chamonix or the Oberland was mostly written on the assumption that the reader would not himself have been there. For this reason the Romantics inclined, one may feel, to pitch it rather high. Later generations have tamed the idea of the Alps, and when Wordsworth speaks of

> *the sick sight*
> *And giddy prospect of the raving stream,*

and Shelley and Coleridge write, like a German band, about the horrors of Mont Blanc, it seems reasonable to suppose that they were whipping out new absolutes of terror and excitement for readers who had tired of their local scene and did not mind how heavily the poet leaned upon the horrors of the unknown. This poetry of sensation has been replaced in our own time by poetry about mountaineering—as when Hardy, standing before the Schreckhorn, "had a vivid sense of him (Leslie Stephen) as if his personality informed the mountain—gaunt and difficult, like himself". Verses of this kind are usually restricted, in area, to the best-known climbing areas, and the best and most poetical notes in English on the Valais are those made by Gerard Manley Hopkins at the age of twenty-four. Descriptions of scenery are nearly always tedious; those writers who, like myself, have no gift for them and tend to skip them in the work of others, are put to shame by the notes of Hopkins; such is the intensity, the supernatural keenness of a true poet's eye. Poets, like painters, look harder and closer than ordinary travellers. Here is Hopkins, on July 20th, 1868, driving down the Rhône valley near Visp. "The churches here have those onion steeples, nearly all the onion being in some cases newly covered with bright tin or lead. They remind me of tinselled humming-tops, too. They enclose the head of the cross in a triangle very commonly: it looks like a beacon at sea. Soon we saw the vines trellised. Hemp swaying in its sweet-smelling thick-set beds; that sprayed silvery weed something like tamarisk leaned over the road—what is it? Maize very high. Spanish chestnuts: their inscape here bold, jutty, somewhat oak-like, attractive, the branching visible, and the leaved peaks spotted so as to make crests of eyes."

So arresting are the bed of the Rhône and its auxiliary valleys that it is easy to forget that the Valais also includes Zermatt, a great part of the St. Bernard and Grimsel passes, and such statutory excitements as the Rhône glacier. Hopkins has described some of them so well that it is now unnecessary, and indeed humiliating (so inferior are one's own perceptions), to visit them. Compare, for instance, the painstaking but trumpery prose of Coxe and Baillie with this: "Walked down to Rhône glacier. It has three stages—first, a smoothly moulded bed in a pan or theatre of thorny peaks: swells of ice rising through the snow-sheet and the snow itself tossing and fretting into the sides of the rock walls in spray-like points; this is the first stage of the glaciers generally; it is like bright-plucked water swaying in a pail; second, after a slope nearly covered with landslips of moraine, was a ruck of horned waves steep and narrow in the gut; now in the upper Grindelwald glacier between the bed or highest stage was a descending limb which was like the rude and knotty bossings of a strombus shell; third, the foot, a broad limb opening out and reaching the plain shaped like the fan-fin of a dolphin or a great bivalve shell turned on its face, the flutings in either case being suggested by the crevasses, and the ribs by the risings between them, these being swerved and inscaped strictly to the notion of the mass. The second stage looked at from nearer appeared like a box of plaster of Paris or starch or tooth-paste, a little moist, tilted up and then struck and jarred so that the powder broke and tumbled in shapes and rifts.

"We went into the grotto and also the vault from which the Rhône flows. It looked like a blue tent, and as you went farther in changed to lilac. As you come out, the daylight glazes the groins with gleaming rose-colour. The ice inside has a branchy wire texture. . . . Standing on the glacier, saw the prismatic colours in the clouds, and worth saying what sort of clouds: it was fine shapeless skins of fretted make, full of eyebrows or like linings of curled leaves which one finds in shelved corners of a wood."

Swiss sensations are now so much a matter of habit (those branches in their white gaiters of snow and ice, that sprig of blossom laid across a prospect of Pilatus) that Hopkins seems to be describing some Hesperidean garden of the imagination. Switzerland to-day is like some magnificent courtesan whom an excess of admirations has fatigued; by their very easiness of access, the splendours of the scene have been diminished in the eyes of the delicate traveller. Hopkins travelled at a time when such fastidiousness was unknown. His visions now seem to us more extraordinary even than the country which prompted them. He spent several days in the Monte Rosa and St. Bernard areas, and his notes suggest, better than any picture, the quality of Alpine life. "Across the valley a pretty village, the houses white, deep-eaved, pierced with small square windows at effective distances, and crossed with balconies, and above, a grove of ash or sycamore, or both, sprayed all one way, like water-weed beds in a running stream, very English-looking. Beyond again, in the midst of a slope of meadow slightly pulled like an unsteady and swelling surface of water, some ashes growing in a beautifully clustered 'bouquet'. First fine; then on the road a thunderstorm with hard rain, the thunder musical and like gongs and rolling in great floors of sound. . . . We drove to St. Remy. As we approached it, the hills 'fledged' with larches, which hung in them shaft after shaft like green-feathered arrows."

No painter has ever thrived by painting the Swiss landscape. Few sights are more pitiable than the huge *machines* with which such artists as Hodler and Segantini have toiled to reproduce the obvious attraction of the Alps. The Muse of painting detests these landscapes. "Live we never so spotlessly," wrote Whistler, "still may she turn her back on us, as from time immemorial she has done upon the Swiss in their mountains." "What more worthy people," he goes on, "whose every Alpine gap yawns with tradition, and is stacked with noble story; yet the perverse and scornful one will have nothing of it, and the sons of patriots are left with the clock that turns the mill, and the sudden cuckoo, with difficulty restrained in its box! For this was Tell a hero! For this did Gessler die!" Such is the magic of frontiers that, a mile or two across the Jura, Courbet could paint the most remarkable landscapes of the nineteenth century; but inside that impalpable ring the camera has the better of the easel; the big painters, Holbein, Fuseli, Klee, neglect the world outside their windows, and for once a writer can dare to outdo the painter at his own trade. Hopkins, at least, has done so.

With such cadences in one's head it would be imprudent to attempt any further account of the natural charms of the Valais. The print of Man, however, may still be profitably deciphered. The Valais is not outstandingly rich in monuments; St. Maurice, for example, is the oldest of Swiss abbeys, but it cannot begin to compare with the magnificence of Einsiedeln and St. Gall; but for those who care to seek them out there are curious and memorable buildings of every period. Swiss architecture has an elasticity of outlook which one cannot hope to find in England. What English town council would have sanctioned, for instance, the church built at Finhaut, in 1925–31, by Fernand Dumas? And the circular church at Saas-Balen would certainly by now have been pulled down. This singular but successful edifice was erected in 1809–12 by J. J. Andermatten, the architect of the Jesuitenkirche in Sion. With its arcaded portico, late baroque decoration, flattened domes and crowning onion, this church should tempt the tourist bound for Saas-Fee to dismount from his mule. It is not far from the more celebrated Kapelle zur Hohen Stiege, near Saas-Fee; this is admired for its position and for the arcaded entrance designed by Antoni Ruppen in 1747.

These are, however, the delicacies of travel, rather than its regular fare. The towns and larger monuments of the Valais are mostly quite modest and rather plain in style. Of the Roman, Burgundian and Savoyard occupations, little now remains: a few strongpoints, some fragments of statuary and the vestiges of larger constructions, now gone beyond recapture, powdered and atomised beneath the surface of the valley. But the Valais has been Christian since the fourth century, and there survive a few buildings which, unlike the abbey at St. Maurice, have remained more or less in their original state since the eleventh and twelfth centuries. The little romanesque church at St. Pierre de Clages is the most remarkable of these, and I cannot sufficiently recommend a visit to where this church lies, baked and roasted by seven centuries of sunshine, among the vineyards on the north bank of the Rhône. The seven centuries have not been so kind to the paintings in the interior of the church, but this is none the less a building which proves that a commanding grandeur can be secured as much by scale as by size. The barn- or garage-like exterior of the west end leads unexpectedly to an octagonal,

46 Saas-Balen : the Round Church (1809-12; *architect J. J. Andermatten*) *(right)*

47 Reckingen : the Church Interior (1743-6; *architect, J. G. Ritz*; *stucco-work by Matthäus Carlen*)

CHURCHES OF THE VALAIS

48   Magadino : with its late Baroque Church of 1845

49   Wiler in the Lötschental

many-lighted tower and a tiled steeple—the whole being completed by
as plucky a cluster of apses as one could wish to find. Elsewhere there
is more fragmentary evidence of the taste of those who ruled in ancient
times over this people of farmers, carters and lodging-house keepers.
The palace of the prætor Asclepiodotus at Sion may have vanished,
but we have the plans, at any rate, of the bathrooms left by the
Romans at Martigny, and we have in many cases the marble floors
and the hypocaustic tiles with which the invaders enlivened their
homes. Pierre II of Savoy built the imposing strongposts which survive, in varying stages of dilapidation, at Martigny, Saillon and
Saxon. If there is not a great deal more, it is perhaps because not
until 1475 did the Valais achieve any degree of political coherence,
and still more because this canton has never fathered those paragons
of industry and self-assertion whose privilege it is to found, in other
provinces and countries, the civic splendours of Birmingham, let us
say, or Lyons, or Philadelphia. Big business is unknown in the
Valais, and for all that half the luxuries of the world must at one time
have passed along the valley of the Rhône, only one man, Gaspard
Stockalper, ever became really rich in the Valais.

Only in the early sixteenth century did an architect impose any
personal style upon Valaisian building. A native of the Val Sesia,
near Monte Rosa, Ulrich Ruffiner had been an apt pupil of the stone-
hewing masons of his time; and he was the pioneer virtuoso of the
distinctive material of the Valais—the calcareous tufa, quarried at
Aproz and Eisscholberg. In 1513 he came to live at Rarogne, where,
with a rare sense of the drama inherent in the long gallery of the
Rhône valley, he built at the summit of a conical hill the wind-
grieved church in which Rilke is buried. This, like much of his work,
was commissioned by Cardinal Schinner, for whom Ruffiner became
indispensable as architect, engineer and general building-adviser.
Under his ægis was built, or rather continued, the Church of St.
Theodule at Sion; only a part of his grandiose scheme had been
completed when Schinner, having backed the wrong side at Marignano, ran into financial difficulties, and Ruffiner's plans were
abandoned. His work may also be seen in the churches at Glis
and Ernen, and in the slaughterhouse at Naters. A decadent Gothic
practitioner, he yields in fashionable interest to that curious colloca-
tion of talent which descended, some two hundred years later, upon
the Ritz family. A short excursion into the Rhône Valley between
Brigue and Münster will reveal many aspects of their art. Selkingen,
some four miles from Münster, was the birthplace of John Ritz
(1668–1729), whose work as sculptor and altar-builder may be seen,
not only there (in the house in which he was born), but at Ritzingen,

Biel, Blitzingen and Oberwald. At Reckingen there is perhaps the
finest late baroque church in the Valais (47); this was built in
1743–5 from plans by John George Ritz, the second son of Johan
Ritz, who was not only an architect and a sculptor, but also the in-
cumbent of the church which he himself had designed. His work as
woodcarver may be seen in the church at Münster; and the Pfarrhaus
in that town is credited by Dr. Jenny with a cupboard by this same
versatile hand. The villages of this valley are mostly primitive constructions of larchwood, and it is surprising to come, at Hohfluh,
Mörel, Teisch, Gluringen and Geschinen, upon churches which are
either wholly baroque inventions dating from between 1660 and
1750, or the repository of altars in the style of the Ritzschule.
Thorough-minded admirers of this family must not neglect the
worth of Johan Jost Ritz, another son of the original monumental
sculptor, whose altars may be seen, in the neighbouring canton of
Uri, at Silenen, Wiler, Wassen, Dörfli, Färnirgen and Göschenealp.

Mühlibach, though near both Ernen and Niederwald, cannot
claim a place in our sculptural and architectural tour. No welcoming
white onion soars above its wooden eves; this village (the colour of
French tobacco) can boast, however, of being the birthplace in 1465
of Cardinal Mathieu Schinner, who more than any other man is the
hero of the Valais. Schinner is a national, not an international, hero.
By Gordon or Kitchener standards, his behaviour at Marignano was
rather disreputable; but he was a power-politician, and in his deter-
mination to strengthen his country he adopted the methods and
the conscience of a Mongolian satrap. Swiss history has clamped
upon his prominent nose, low forehead and unsmiling mouth the
mask of a hero; and he combined, with the normal tenacity of the
Valaisan, the form of ambition which, though now blessed by tradition, is in reality the most savage of human appetites. "He was as
cunning and as obstinate as a peasant," writes Gonzague de Reynold.
"Often he forgot those who had helped and served him; but he
drove every slight into his memory, as one drives a rivet into steel
plate. . . . He never let himself be beaten. He for renown, and for
profit; coming of a poor race, he knew the value of gold, and he was
sustained until the day of his death by one great thought." This
great thought has survived in the hearts of his countrymen, for whom
the example of his undaunted upward thrust remains the most potent
of inspirations.

It is natural that Schinner should be associated with Sion, but this
extraordinary town is in no danger of becoming swamped in the
celebrity of its most famous citizen. The physiognomy of Sion (40)
is independent of all that the human race can do to change it; the two

great humps, with their smaller fellow, the stony mattress of the encircling Rhône, and on either side the high mountain-ramparts— all these are much as they were in 57 B.C., when Galba's legions took over the town. Not until the Augustan era did the Roman armies finally settle in Sion; but when they did come, it was for more than four hundred years; many were the Romans who married in Sion, and many were they who chose to retire there. The Pax Romana was more than a phrase in the Valais. Not only did the Romans bring peace, but they taught the Sedunois how to live, how to make the most of their scanty soil, how to plant vines and fruit trees, how to make wine. It is to the Augustan legions that, in the last resort, we owe the Johannisberg Mont d'Or and the Fendant de Sion.

Sion to-day comprises elements of every architectural period. It is not a town which people have taken great care of; it has been there a long time, in the sun and in the dry (Sion has the lowest rainfall in Switzerland), and only recently has it been regarded as a town of architectural interest. Even Dr. Jenny asserts that the Cathedral (51), which lies just off the dusty, uneven Place de la Planta, is "no dis-play-place, in the accepted sense". This could not be said of Notre-Dame de Valère. A fortified church of the twelfth and thirteenth centuries, several hundred feet up in the air, is certainly a display-place, and well worth the climb. On the sister hump, the bishop's palace of Tourbillon has been left roughly as it was after the great fire of 1788. From either, one can hover in imagination, like Asmo-deus, above the drowsing town—envisaging the successive stages of its development: the monumental tower of the Cathedral, so evoca-tive of the time when to build at all was to build with grandeur; Ruffiner's St. Theodule, beloved of Schinner; the Maison Super-saxo, rue de Conthey 153, built by the great family who first en-couraged Schinner, and whose kindness he later betrayed; the Hôtel de Ville (1660–61), in which one may examine the inscription which proves that by 377 the Romans in Sion had been converted to Christianity; the Church of the Jesuits, built in 1809 by J. J. Andermatten—the last resonance, one might say, of the rococo; along the rue de Savièse, the elegant town-houses run up by the aristocracy of Sion immediately after the fire of 1788; and every-where, the sure mark of Sion—light and elegant balconies of wrought iron.

Sion is a beautiful town, but stifling. The visitor may well decide to mount in search of air—into the Val d'Hérémence, for instance, as far as the Mayens de Pralong; or he may go east, into the Lötschental (49). This is one of the grandest and least accessible of Swiss mountain valleys. The extreme difficulty of getting into it at all has saved it from exploitation, and indeed there is much about it which suggests some magical or allegorical landscape—the glacier grottoes at the foot of the Tennbachhorn, the silent avalanches of powdered snow which can crush a house by the mere pressure of moving air, the galena mines which once, it is said, were streaked with silver, the hundred-year-old cheeses at Ferden, and the painted wooden crosses (blue for husbands and wives, black for those who remained single) in the churchyard at Kippel. Only recently has the valley been known to visitors. In 1799 an officer from the Vaud described it as "a little Siberia, with its bears, chamois, marmots and half-wild population". Not for another seventy or eighty years was the Lötschental valued for its example of a society in which nothing had changed for many generations; in which there was no tavern, no gambling, no variation of dress or employment, and everybody was dressed in cloth woven from his own sheep. Within doors, friezes of carved wood took the place of pictures, and master-craftsmen from Lucerne and the Unterwald came to work in the seventeenth century on the houses overlooking the square at Ferden. This is the country, too, in which are made some of the most fantastic and disturbing of Swiss peasant-masks. The faculty of wonder, so rarely preserved intact in more sophisticated communities, is very strong in the Lötschental, and nowhere are the cycle of the Roman Catholic year, and the simple festivals of communal life, more vividly and enthusiastically followed. The mercenary tradition of soldiering is still very much alive in the valley, and on the great festival of Segensonntag the old uniforms of the armies of France, Spain and Naples are brought out of storage and a great parade is held. Nowhere does wind music sound finer than in this aerial fastness. So strong, moreover, is the tradition of acting in the Lötschental that each village has had for many years its own dramatic society; *Hamlet* and *Macbeth*, for instance, are among the plays which have been acted at Wiler.

To get into or out of the Lötschental, it is best to go by Brigue. This little town is one of the great junctions of Switzerland—is, indeed, all that many travellers ever see of the Valais. I shall not encourage my readers to leap out of the Simplon Express in order to scour Brigue at leisure, but I do attest the pleasure to be had by arriving in one's motor—pausing on the way to examine the magnificent church at Glis (Ruffiner's masterpiece, later embellished with a sumptuous baroque gateway)—and putting up at the Couronne et Poste. This hotel, like the Hôtel de l'Europe at Avignon, has preserved the atmosphere of more leisurely times, and from it one can observe, undisturbed, the animation of the square. Brigue exists mainly as a springboard for the Simplon Pass; the huge Stockalper

50   The Château de Valère

51   The Cathedral of Notre-Dame

SION

52   Zürich : the Lindenhof in Winter

Palace serves to point the way, and in its architecture there is already something of the dramatic sense, the assertion of individuality, which make an Italian town so memorably alive. As Cingria has remarked, there is something "tautened and accelerated" about Brigue. One must not exaggerate: the quarter round the station has the authentic Swiss dullness; but if the main square does not suggest the background for an unknown opera of Verdi, it does at any rate suggest an English production of that masterpiece.

IV

Zürich and the Zürichsee

CIRCUMSTANCES have given Zürich a new importance in European life. With the destruction or temporary insignificance of such great towns as Munich, Leipzig and Dresden, there exists no more active and fully equipped centre of Germanic culture. Zürich, which has always valued, and sometimes been able to foster, the German contribution to literature, science, philosophy and music, has recently been the only city in which these may still be studied in tolerable conditions. It cannot pretend to replace, in its outward appearance, the vanished marvels of Würzburg, Heilbronn, Trier and Ulm—let alone the splendid masses of inspired building which put Munich and Dresden among the wonders of the world. Such things cannot be duplicated, and Zürich has always been a city in which brilliance, or indeed marked personality of any kind, has been regarded as untypical of Zürcher life. Lavater, for example, was never quite assimilated; and when, in the late fifteenth century, the city fostered a statesman of downright pragmatic ability, the citizens soon decided to cut off his head. Zürich has always been strenuously independent; and the independence of the Middle Ages, the struggles to get free of the Abbey of Fraumünster and the Counts of Zähringen, were later replaced by independences of other kinds. One historian has remarked that the prime fact about Zürich is that it has never had a reigning aristocracy and has on the contrary expressed the aspirations of a successful but never tyrannical business community. The chronic independence of Zürich includes, in short, the right to suspect any personal hegemony. Between 1078 and 1802 Zürich endured a considerable number of sieges; and one of them (that of 1354) was a very formidable affair; but, for all that, there never arose in the city a military caste of any importance. Trade was the thing; soldiering was bad for trade—between 1357 and 1467, when the soldiers were busy with wars against Austria and the Confederate, the city sickened for lack of trade and lost two-thirds of its population. Such a mistake was never made again, and since the sixteenth century business has ruled in Zürich. It rules to-day, and what might have been a little town at the head of a lake the northern counterpart of Thun or Zug, is the largest and most prosperous city in Switzerland. Travel-snobbery has often insinuated that Zürich is the Swiss equivalent of Bradford or Lille; and it

86

is true that its two finest monuments, the Grossmünster (53, 54) and the Fraumünster, date from the time when Zürich was a royal, and not a bourgeois, city. There are not many admired buildings in Zürich, and it is certainly not one of those mummified *villes d'art* to which the conscientious tourist must accord, willy-nilly, a tribute of respectful attention. But there can be few cities in which it is so agreeable to live, and in which the sense of the past is so well nourished by the adventures of the present. Every good European must like Zürich; for only in Zürich can one now recapture the disinterested intellectual speculation which was once the blazon of German enlightenment. It needs no perception to notice this in 1950; but Paul Valéry—and no one in the twentieth century has more finely served the ideal of Europe—remarked it twenty-five years earlier. Valéry responded, as all must do, to many aspects of Zürich: the huge clock-faces, royal-blue and gold, of the churches between the Sihl and the Limmat; the watermen's poles, striped blue-and-white in the colours of the city; the ancient houses on the Schipfe with their back-gardens on the level of the third-floor window; and the golden helmets of the Grossmünster. But he was a person for whom art could be enriched with the nerveless exactitude of science, and science dignified, in its turn, with the Promethean audacity of art; in Zürich he saluted a city where experience and speculation were held in equal honour. His admiration was kindled as much by the laboratories of the Zürich Polytechnic, where savants are for ever in search of "the new phenomenon, the unforeseen idea", as by the many-bowered Villa Wesendonck, in which Wagner conceived and constructed the encounter of Tristan and Isolde. "There are many other things at Zürich," Valéry wrote; "but each one of us is sensitive above all to what awakens his most private weaknesses, and I have few others than this—my hunger for everything that excites in me the idea of intellectual activity."

As Valéry went on to remark, the engineer, the industrialist, the banker and the man of affairs can all find matter, in Zürich, for astonishment and admiration; but the simple tourist may prefer to draw on a small part of Valéry's great store of intellectual curiosity, and to interpret Zürich as the city which Wagner, Lenin, James Joyce, Einstein, Paul Klee and C. G. Jung have dowered with a unique tradition of creative activity.

The scientific tradition of Zürich dates broadly from the Reformation. If Zwingli and his successor Heinrich Bullinger are the heroes of the religious history of the city, Konrad Gesner may be called the founder of the tradition of which Einstein and Jung are the contemporary ornaments. Gesner was two years old when, in 1519,

Zwingli preached his first public sermon in Zürich. He had no advantages of rank or fortune; nor had he the sort of cunning, low but necessary, with which scholars sometimes contrive to secure leisure and security for their studies. Gesner was always in want; his time was always being wasted in menial literary commissions; and yet, in his forty-seven years, he applied himself with revolutionary effect to the study of philology, bibliography, therapeutics, surgery, gynæcology, natural history and botany. Ourselves live in an age of specialization, when the study of one phase in the work of a minor artist of the Seicento is regarded as the honourable and sufficient occupation of a lifetime, and many scholars are more interested in scoring off one another than in reproducing the naïve, panoramic interests of the Renaissance. Merely to enumerate the subjects of which Gesner made himself the master is to conceive the inadequacy of current standards. His *Mithridate*, published in 1555 and based on his studies of French, German, Italian, Dutch, Latin, Greek, Hebrew and Arabic, was a pioneer work in the comparative study of language. Ten years earlier he had published, at the age of twenty-nine, his *Bibliotheca Universalis*, an annotated bibliography of all books of any importance (in Greek, Latin and Hebrew) from the earliest times. To this he added, by way of appendix, a catalogue of over 30,000 generic terms. These labours remained for three centuries the foundation of all bibliographical studies. As a practising doctor, Gesner could rarely boast a patient; but as a theorist he was indefatigable, and his *Precious Treasury of Remedies* was translated into many languages and ran through more than twenty editions. He only had time, as naturalist, to publish four stout volumes on the mammals, amphibians, reptiles, saurians, quadrupeds, birds and aquatic animals; but zoology, in these volumes, is traced to its farthest sources. Gesner had intended to follow them with a Treatise on Botany. No desk-man, he had carried out researches for this in the highest Alps, and had plunged beneath the surface of his native rivers and lakes. In the last year of his life he published a separate study of fossils. Almost with exasperation, indeed, must one record the fact that Gesner illustrated his botanical studies with drawings from his own hand. Like his great compatriot Paracelsus, he gave a new and grandiose stature to human curiosity; but unlike that vagabond genius, he disliked leaving home. Zürich was world enough for him; and his heroic, not to say daunting, example has remained the supreme symbol of Zürcher industry.

Gesners are not found twice. In the eighteenth century, however, Gesner's encyclopædic curiosity became diffused throughout Zürich, and the city as a whole became a stronghold of the Enlightenment.

Learned societies were founded, and a fruitful amateurism drove citizens of every kind to take part in the exercises of the mind. One man can be named as the motor force in this development—Jean-Jacques Bodmer. To him, too, is due the firmly Germanic cast of most of these studies. Bodmer was, from 1731 until his death in 1783, Professor of Swiss History at the Academy of Zürich, and much of his energies were given to the study and propagation of the history of the Confederates; in these noble ancestors he found the simplicity and plain strength of mind which he hoped to perpetuate in his pupils. It was he who reintroduced Dante to German readers, who translated the whole of the *Iliad* and the whole of *Paradise Lost*, and who sponsored the first German translation of Shakespeare. With his lifelong friend J. J. Breitinger, he made Zürich nothing less than the temporary intellectual capital of Europe; and visitors as imposing as Goethe and the Grand Duke of Saxe-Weimar were made welcome in Bodmer's little house in the Schönbergergasse. Lavater and Fuseli were among his admirers, and Fuseli painted a conversation-piece in which he himself, glassy from too much listening, is addressed by Bodmer, with didactic forefinger outstretched to secure attention; a yet greater Ancient, revived by the sculptor's art, presides over the interview. In Bodmer, the intermediary genius of the Swiss mind finds almost its finest expression; and never has the geographical position of Zürich been used to better advantage. A new Bodmer could to-day make Zürich once again the headquarters of German literature.

The rôle of the intermediary is one to which few young men aspire; but, as I have hinted already, the civic spirit of Zürich is not favourable to men of imaginative genius. When Bodmer, for example, invited Klopstock to stay, he found that the author of "The Messiah" was by no means the amenable angel whom he had envisaged; and Klopstock for his part had no taste for the simple earnestness of Zürcher life. It is the privilege of Zürich to transmit, one would think, rather than to initiate. Did not Goethe say of the great publishing house of Gesner and Orell Füssli that it "had done more service to literature than half the publishers in Germany"? Our judgment must be arrested, however, by the apparition, towards 1760, of the poet-painter Salomon Gessner. Here, for once, the city looked kindly upon a creative artist. The son of a publisher, Gessner was able to exploit his gifts as poet and illustrator in a series of books which must be among the most homogeneous creations in the history of publishing. When he revealed himself, moreover, as the originator of a new way of looking at nature, the city rose to its opportunity and made him Master of its Forests. Gessner's work is saturated with an untroubled happiness; its notes are too high, and perhaps too thin, to carry across to our own time, but in the poems of André Chénier, and through Chénier in much of the French Romantic movement, there is diffused the tiny twang of this exquisite artist. Even Chateaubriand, weariest and most difficult of travellers, who detested most of Zürich, could not but exempt from blame "the memory of Gessner, the trees of an esplanade which dominates the lake, the banks of the Limmat, an ancient crow and an ancient elm".

The talents of Fuseli are now so highly esteemed in England that I shall not presume to introduce them to my readers. At most shall I urge them to make their way up the Kirchgasse to the Kunsthaus, where his works may be studied in profusion (this gallery, like that at Basle, is one of the most interesting in Europe, and it is one of the very few public galleries in which contemporary painting may be studied before it has gone off the boil); but the disordered night-world of Fuseli cannot be related to the history of his native city, and remains a suggestive but isolated fancy. The character of Zürich can be studied more profitably in the work of Gottfried Keller.

Keller was to the nineteenth century what Ramuz has been to the twentieth—the worthy embodiment, that is to say, of Switzerland as foreigners see her. Like many eminent Zürchers, Keller served his native city alike in public and in private; like Usteri the naturalist, and Conrad Escher the engineer and Conrad de Muralt the historian and man of affairs, he gladly gave much of his time to public work, and for fifteen years was secretary to the cantonal government. Yet it is not for this that he is most honoured, but for the art with which, during a long career as novelist, poet and story-writer, he made the Swiss way of life a recognizable ideal for all German-speaking peoples. It is not too much to say that Keller prefigured the fortunate turn of history by which Swiss public life has become a model of harmonious efficiency. Writers tend, of course, to exaggerate the influence of literature upon public affairs; but there is a sense in which traditions do not exist until someone has given them memorable expression, and nearly all the things for which we are most grateful in modern Switzerland are foreshadowed in Keller's long novel, *Der Grüne Heinrich*. His recommendations seem now almost otiose, and one has to remember, as he preaches the willing subjection of the individual to the interests of the group, that he wrote at a time when the equilibrium of the Swiss state was anything but assured. Keller lived in Zürich for sixty of his seventy years, and his work is saturated in the city and in the countryside around it; but his services were rendered to a wider ideal—that of

53 Zürich : the Limmatquai and the Grossmünster

54 Zürich : the Zunfthaus zur Meise (1752 ; *architect, David Morf*),
with the Grossmünster and the Fraumünster

the Federal State of Switzerland, whose constitution dates only from 1848. Keller was then in his thirtieth year, and unknown as a writer. That he would eventually be acclaimed as one of the greatest German writers of the nineteenth century must have seemed implausible; that he should have achieved it in Switzerland, and by lifelong devotion to Swiss subjects, gave a new dignity to the rejuvenated state.

Keller was a very small man—so short, indeed, that his chairlegs were specially shortened to give him free access to the ground. Abashed, in early youth, by a sense of his own insignificance, and being in any case quite speechless by temperament, he remained an eternal bachelor; but he was none the less a man of unusually powerful affections, and these he discharged, not only upon the varied and exquisite phantoms of femininity who haunt his stories and poems, but upon his native countryside. One could not do better, indeed, than tour Zürich in the footsteps of the diminutive bard—beginning at his birthplace, Zum Goldenen Winkel in the Neumarkt, next the Predigerkirche. It is in these narrow streets on the far side of the Limmat that much of his life was passed—in childhood at the Haus zur Sichel in the Rindermarkt, where a ditch-like backgarden served as hen-run, tool-house and summer retreat, and in the square tower of the Steinhaus (33 Kirchgasse), where Keller had his offices as Staatsschreiber. It is in these precipitous alleys, with their fan-set cobbles, green shutters and wide eaves, that the best food in Zürich is still to be found; in these twilit *antiquaires*, the best furniture and the rarest books; and in the almost stationary life of the whole quarter, the most bizarre and rewarding encounters. For this is innermost Zürich; here the city began. On the eminence which now the Grossmünster adorns, worship of some sort has been celebrated since prehistoric times; and as we puff up or down the Kirchgasse the aerial headnotes of invisible choristers remind us that we have omitted to scrutinize the great church to which the waterfront owes all that is august in its character.

Like Switzerland itself, the Grossmünster (53, 54) is a mixture which, with age, has shaken down rather well. Time has dismissed, for example, the splendidly barbaric statue of Charlemagne from the south tower (where it had been since 1472) and sent it to skulk in the crypt (a copy still squats high on the south tower). The west front, which lies aslant the Limmat and is approached by a gentle ramp, is Romanesque in its three lower storeys, late Gothic (1487–92) in the two above and neo-Gothic (1778–82) in the topmost towers. Victor Hugo called these last "ignoble pepper-pots", and it is possible to regret the twin spires which appear in Meryan's engraving and were struck by lightning in 1763; but those who have lived in

91

Zürich would not lightly forfeit the golden domes. The interior of the Grossmünster is also the product of successive, and sometimes contradictory, inspirations. The low arch which separates the nave from the chancel is a witness to these, for it was originally intended that the chancel ceiling should consist of two massive cross-vaults, while the nave was to have a flat wooden ceiling on a slightly higher level. About 1170, however, the success of S. Ambrogio in Milan encouraged the building, on Milanese lines, of a triforium above the aisles. The effect of this was, of course, to darken the nave; after fifty years of penumbra the nave walls were raised and the present clerestory inserted; the nave was then vaulted and the chancel ceiling raised in proportion. In our own generation the Minster has been ornamented by the addition of Augusto Giacometti's windows in the choir, and by Otto Bänninger's statue of Bullinger (by the north-west door).

The drowsing, wedge-packed quarter between the Grossmünster and the Kunsthaus (54) is not, of course, the only curiosity on the east bank of the Limmat. There are the mansions along the Rämi-strasse (note especially No. 18, built c. 1750), and behind them, Dolder-wards, terraces of villas, each struggling for its view of the city and the lake. Down at the water's edge, again, there is the pleasure-quarter. This is not the most successful part of Zürich; the Swiss character does not lend itself to sophisticated amusement, and there is in these dim-lit saloons a peculiar heaviness, a lack of abandon which must chill the heart of all but the most intrepid reveller. (One English visitor, in 1837, described Zürich as "a city where amusement is confounded with crime".) There are, in Zürich, cinemas of the *avant-garde*, in which one may seek out the films of Dreyer and Pabst, and others in which a Bette-Davis-Zyklus, or a chronological review of films by Orson Welles, will gratify the systematic admirer of these artists. As for the Stadttheater, there are not many cities in which one can count on seeing operas by Eugen d'Albert, Weber and Janacek along with the favourites of the international repertory, but Zürich is one of them. The theatre itself is an ill-ventilated building of the 1890s, but it has those prime re-quirements of the good opera-house—a large orchestra pit and plenty of boxes. Along the Utoquai (55) and the Seefeldquai, there is a promenade which could be removed, without loss of congruity, to Ostend or Scheveningen; but the view is Zürich's own—Turnerian, as a rule, with spectral towers athwart a shifting wall of mist.

Once across the Limmat, all is changed. This is the quarter of Zürich which sensitive persons are said to shrink from penetrating, on the ground that it is too gross, too material to engage their sympathies. It is here that a great commercial city does the greater part of its business, and it is precisely this tremendous material development which keeps the whole of Zürich in such excellent trim. Two things redeem this part of the city and save it from the fate of such comparable cities as Bradford and Middlesbrough. First, it was not burdened in the nineteenth century with gigantic capital expenditure in the form of cumbrous and now obsolete heavy industrial equipment; its industries are recent and relatively light, so that even in the thickest industrial area Zürich is never an oppressive city. Second, the city has never been seedy; its activities have been wisely spread over a wide range of industry, and it has none of those hideous quarters which elsewhere betray the disappearance of favour. Switzerland is not a country in which the sores of the past lie open. Much of Zürich is ugly, but it is never the reckless, uncaring ugliness of other countries; and if there are places in Switzerland in which human beings should not be allowed to live, they are not—as far as my experience allows me to judge—in the large towns, but in the remote hamlets of the Grisons and the Ticino.

The west bank of the Limmat is frankly a business-man's town. Hotel lobbies here carry only the sober cards of the professional middleman; restaurants, without being very good, adapt their prices to the expansive humour of the executive whose expenses are paid by his firm; and at midday there is the habitual scramble of the competitive city. The centre of all this is, of course, the Bahnhofstrasse, along which the trams run as if threaded with a needle, and where the double line of trees is disregarded, for nobody has the time to seek their shade. It is a street of the kind for which Haussmann is finally responsible, but it serves its purpose very well. If it had not been built, the great office-blocks would have spread horizontally, not vertically, and the many charming streets between it and the Limmat would have been destroyed. As it is, the river-marge, with its footpath, narrow as a bosun's ladder, is still intact; No. 49 Schipfe has still its oriel, than which there are few finer in Switzerland; no novelties deface the leafy little eminence of the Lindenhof; and even the Augustinergasse is unspoilt, with its baroque elegances at Nos. 19, 25 and 28. It is in these streets and squares that the ideal of quality is kept alive. Around the Fraumünster there are more massive reminders of the past—the great Zunfthaus zur Meise (54) shows that the influence of France, against which in the eighteenth century J. J. Bodmer threw all his weight, had made little headway in the field of architecture. This building, and its companion the Rechberg (in the Hirschengraben, on the other bank of the Limmat), were built between 1750 and 1770 by

David Morf, who was the best Zürcher architect of the period. Not for an instant do these careful erections come alive, but they are the nearest thing, in Zürich, to an aristocratic style. (It is interesting, after visiting the Rechberg, which Morf built for Caspar Werdmüller-Oeri, to examine the Pension Florhof, in the adjacent Florhofgasse, which Morf designed for Werdmüller-Oeri's coachman.)

Reverting to the Bahnhofstrasse and the tall, faceless buildings which compose it, we who rather enjoy it all can take comfort from the example of James Joyce, and turn to the page, in *Pomes Penyeach*, on which he paid his tribute to the derided street. This poem is not one of great consequence; if I do not quote it, it is for fear that I might misrepresent, by printing a poem of four couplets, the man who is the greatest twentieth-century master of large-scale literary forms. The difficulty of *Ulysses*, for example, has been so grossly exaggerated that it is known, even now, only to a small number of readers. Not, perhaps, for another fifty years will it become common property; but meanwhile we can be proud that an English-speaking writer should have given a new turn to the mythology of Zürich. Joyce was a predominantly urban writer, and the large town or small city was his favourite unit of society—so much so that, as his friend Madame Giedion-Welcker has recorded, he thought it more important, more satisfying, "more organic" to be mayor of a town than king of a nation. Zürich was, next to Dublin, the city which most perfectly suited his taste. He first went there on his honeymoon, in 1904, and stayed at the Hôtel Speer, Lagerstrasse 16. In 1915 he returned to Zürich from Trieste, where he had been living with his wife and their two children. He stayed for four years; and it is to this period, when he supported his family by giving English lessons in the Berlitz School, that some of the finest passages in *Ulysses* may be traced. The Joyces lived on the east bank of the Limmat—in the Kreuzstrasse, the Seefeldstrasse (behind the Stadttheater), and the Universitätstrasse, which runs from the University to the Rigiviertel funicular. His friends have recounted some of the things which particularly bound him to Zürich—a taste for the Fendant de Sion, which he drank every evening in the Pfauen or the Kronenhalle restaurants; admiration for those ingenious and lively beings, the hall-porters of Zürich's hotels, and gratitude for the company of humane and appreciative friends. For Joyce, who taught the English language a new cantilena, an opera-house was the first necessity of an important town; and, like Wagner, he tried to intervene in the practical world of the theatre. Wagner's *The Theatre in Zürich* failed of its effect; but Joyce's *English Players* did

55 Zürich from the Utoquai

56 Altstätten, near St. Gall: eighteenth-century arcaded houses

at least perform plays by Wilde, Shaw and Synge in Zürich and Lucerne, and one must presume that a few Zürchers took fire from his enthusiasm, since in 1948 Zürich beat London to the post by giving the first performance of Mr. Shaw's *Buoyant Billions*. Joyce was alive, too, to the mysterious possibilities of Zürich's natural situation—between a lake, a mountain and two rivers; he took great pleasure in the submarine life of the lake; and, most of all, he responded to the great Zürich festival of the Sechseläuten. This occurs each year on a Monday in mid-April, when a symbolic figure of winter is ceremoniously burnt in the centre of the Bellevue Platz. The spring festivals of Roman times, so long trodden into the footnotes of history, come momentarily alive as the Zürchers, warmed by the Sechseläuten march, perform their polite variants of an antique cult; and, with them, is revived a later tradition—that of the city, as dominated by its Guilds; it is on Sechseläuten night that *Die Meistersinger* (much of it written in Zürich) moves forward from the proscenium arch and becomes a part of ordinary life.

To Joyce, so great a lover of all festivals, Zürich on such a day was doubly of value; and one can conceive with what relief he arrived at the Hauptbahnhof on December 13th, 1940. Fresh from the Byzantine intrigues of Vichy, he was well placed to appreciate the amenities of Swiss life. "Here", he remarked in his hotel, "we still know where we stand." We must be grateful that his last few weeks were spent in the city of which he was so fond, and where he had encountered, in the person of one of his pupils, some of the idiosyncrasies which later were blended in the character of Leopold Bloom —the greatest comic creation in English literature since Falstaff.

Joyce was grateful to the last; but not all of Zürich's guests have shown such fineness of feeling. I do not know that Lenin, for example, ever spoke very kindly of the highly capitalized community which gave him asylum; and as for Wagner—the ingratitude of this illustrious shade makes painful reading. Zürich, in his view, was "a desert. I shall rot away here," he continued, "and everything will come too late, too late!" He was not really content until he got outside the city, to the Villa Wesendonck, or even to the Haus Mariafeld in Meilen. This may seem, to more mundane spirits, a confusion of taste, for there is not a great deal in the country round Zürich to compare with the planturous outskirts of Basle and Berne, so rich in fine country houses. The bourgeois traditions of Zürich have never lent themselves to irrelevant display, and the Zürichsee, as if in sympathy, is curiously drab. In recent years the lakeside has become littered, it is true, with sumptuous villas; but the simple tourist will get little comfort from these, as he glumly picks his way from factory to factory, or swims out in desperation to those sandy, urine-scented islands which so signally do not repay a close inspection. Let him but persevere, however, as far as Horgen, on the south bank, and he will see one of the most curious buildings in Switzerland—the oval Protestant church built in 1780 by Johann Jakob Haltiner. In this church the simple rectangle of the traditional preaching-room is replaced by—or, to be exact, combined with—the musical curves and elaborate stucco decoration of the Vorarlberg school, and there are even two frescoes which Deschwanden himself could not have bettered. A similar perseverance on the north bank will reveal, at Meilen and at Herrliberg, good specimens of the country houses, large and unpretending, in which the great families of Zürich once spent their leisure. But these are placid enjoyments; one has only to press on to the Wallensee to enjoy one of the most exciting lakes in Europe. Almost vertical screes rise from its surface to a height of several thousand feet; the scene has been called gloomy, and in winter can be so; but in summer there are few more exhilarating sights than to stand on the upper road and peer down to where the lake lies like a single emerald below. In doing so, one experiences all the familiar Swiss sensations—the limitless but near-seeming distance, the clear brilliance of the air, the foliage smoothed and softened as if by the brush of a Corot; but what is usually dispersed, and insignificant through mere excess of liberty and size, is here concentrated into a single *Blick*; the paddle-steamer hovers like a may-fly above the tiny, luminous oval of the lake, and the whole scene, now purged of its archaic attributes of terror and awe, unites to proffer a moment of the rarest invigoration. Afterwards, other country seems tame, and there is nowhere particular to stay in the neighbourhood. It is best to return in the twilight to Zürich, past the motor yachts and the floating Turkish bath, to where, along the slopes of the Zürichberg, the house-lights are beginning to come out like fireflies. Worldly pleasures are then offered in abundance. One has a choice of twenty-two cinemas, a music-hall or a careful performance of *Volpone* in German-Swiss; in any case, a dinner of salmon-trout and *Leber-spiessli*, and perhaps afterwards a walk along the Limmat, with moonlight to blanch the house-fronts and a few noctambulant swans to beg for alms beneath the Uraniabrücke. Certain buildings gain immensely by the chiaroscuro of moonlight—none more so, for instance, than the Hauptwache, or Guard House, a stronghold in Greek Revival style, rebuilt in 1825 by Caspar Escher; and night is a good time in which to examine the extraordinarily ramshackle group of buildings which stands in the middle of the river just before the Bahnhofbrücke. The survival, in so strenuously modern a city, of this almost derelict construction must be ascribed to some deep strain of antiquarian feeling. Reached by a covered wooden bridge of the seventeenth century, the dilapidated pile offers a commanding view towards the lake; pedlars tempt one with milk chocolate, and with one's change one is offered an uneatable brown fruit, all pips and pith; and within, behind cracked windows, an indefinable commercial activity goes anxiously forward. Night and silence enhance the oddity of this attaching phenomenon. Alas! Progress has overtaken these buildings, and by the time this book appears they will no longer exist.

V

Central Switzerland

Lucerne—Tribschen—Engelberg—The Passes—Andermatt—
Einsiedeln

THERE is nothing really wrong with Lucerne, except the people who go there. The public buildings suffer, perhaps, from an excess of good care, but they include at least two churches which, in any other town, would have become famous. The general defects of life in Lucerne must be ascribed, I am afraid, to a century of English patronage. In fine weather it is still delightful to walk beside the Reuss towards the Spreuerbrücke, and watch the fast-running stream hang like a pad of green velvet above the weir. A fruit-market is never dull, and in the evening it is possible, by exploring beneath the arches along the Rathausquai and Unter der Egg, to find watermen's cafés in which to escape the crippling boredom of the professional pleasure-resort. To taste, however, the full savour of this town one must wait for a wet Sunday afternoon in August, when Lucerne has the air of an industrial Keswick, and the mist hangs like a wet mat on one's shoulders. Then does the English colony show its spirit. Out come the Burberreys and the backward sons; silently and six abreast, chewing their unlit pipes and tucking loose strands of hair into mackintosh hoods, the family parties come out for a tramp. There are cities in which wet weather is positively pleasant, but Lucerne is not among them. Matthew Arnold seized, once and for all, the magical consolations of sunshine at Lucerne, when he described "the blaze of colour now that the rain has brought the purple that was wanted, the bright green still of the pastures, the black green of the firs, the yellow gold of the poplars, walnuts, chestnuts and wych elms, and the red gold of the beeches, and at the foot of it all the lake, and at the head of it all the snowy line with Titlis . . . then Lucerne itself with its curtain of old wall and trees and bridges, and the broad blue-green Reuss going through it. It required a day of mist and rain and penetrating damp . . . to make it possible for one to depart." On such a day it is a good plan to disentangle the early history of Switzerland and to re-wind the skein of events which made the Kapellbrücke, for example, a great staging-point in the development of the country.

This bridge is possibly the best known, among English visitors, of all Swiss monuments. It was built in 1333, and between 1599 and 1611 it was ornamented with nearly a hundred and sixty paintings, by H. H. Wagmann and his son, of scenes from Swiss history; these hang from the gabled roof which stretches the length of the bridge and is only interrupted by the monumental Wasserturm. Broad-angled and hooded, the bridge survives now as a well-liked curiosity; but we can see from the plan in Stumpf's *Schweizerchronik* (1606) that it was formerly part of an elaborate defence-system, with towers and turrets beyond number in the town itself and on the eminence to the north-east. It served, in fact, as a kind of waterborne rampart, and a defence against such naval forays as had been attempted in 1332 by the fleet of the Forest. But 1333 is an important year in Lucerne's history. Eighteen years earlier the battle of Morgarten had been fought, and in this the Habsburgs, with Duke Leopold of Austria at their head, were signally beaten by the Forest Cantons of Switzerland. Lucerne at this time was in bondage to the Habsburgs; although it was the natural market-place of the Cantons, its markets had been forcibly closed to its neighbours, and the town itself no longer flourished. Since the opening of the St. Gotthard Pass, Lucerne had been the point at which all traffic to and from the Pass would naturally assemble. After the battle of Morgarten, the Cantons felt able to challenge a situation which was in the highest degree inconvenient for them. The lake itself, so essential to their communications, was no longer safe for their traffic; indeed, the Habsburgs could paralyse at will the communications by which the Cantons lived. In 1327, when the Cantons formed a coalition of which Berne and Zürich were members, the burghers of Lucerne were given an example of the new spirit which was animating Swiss affairs. Before long they were conspiring to overthrow their masters; in 1330 they effected this, by a revolution classical in its simplicity; and in 1332 they joined in perpetual aliance with Schwyz, Uri and Unterwalden. Thus the building of the Kapellbrücke, at once bridge and rampart, may be said to symbolize the renascence of Lucerne as an important and independent town; and it is not surprising that the oldest layer of Lucerne as we know it is composed of carefully ornamented fourteenth-century Gothic. It is important to recognize, across the peaceable and welcoming façade of the new town, that Lucerne and its lake have nurtured many of the national heroes of the country—not least Tell himself, whose shrine will be familiar to all visitors to the Vierwaldstätter Sea. In the chancel of the Franziskanerkirche, for instance, one may see commemorated the fact that in 1387 men from Lucerne formed the spearhead of the Swiss army at the victory of Sempach, and a soldier from Unterwalden, Arnold von Winkelreid, performed one of those legendary acts upon which later heroes are nourished; it is not surprising that this knight, who gathered into his embrace some thirty Austrian lances before falling dead in the field, should have been adopted as the subject of so many nineteenth-century *tableaux de genre*.

The Spreuerbrücke, which itself dates from 1404, has some fifty-six paintings of the Dance of Death by Kasper Meglinger and one of his contemporaries. The two covered bridges of Lucerne are the principal monuments of their time in the town. The Rathaus was built about 1602 by Anton Isenmann, an architect known for his work on the Cistercian Abbey at Rathausen and the Franciscan Klosterkirche at Werthenstein. It incorporates the tower of an earlier town-hall; the exterior of this was decorated in 1863 with wall paintings of idiosyncratic crudity. The Rathaus itself represents an uneasy coupling of Renaissance and Louis XIII motifs; meticulous restoration has thrown this experiment into undeserved relief. Its interior will be found, however, to contain several weighty and authentic pieces of historical decoration. The Renaissance Lesesaal, for instance, where every panel has its own pediment; the Porträtsaal (1781), with its triple deck of Swiss worthies, landscapes and *scènes de genre*; the Archivraum of 1698, with a heavy gallery carried on columns; and everywhere a great deal of panelling in high relief, and those two great symbols of Swiss comfort and efficiency—the enormous porcelain stove and the municipal clock. From these ponderous chambers it is possible to deduce the watchful and temperate sagacity which has enriched Lucerne (63).

None of these buildings much affects the real character of the town, which is that of an Edwardian watering-place, unaccountably gifted with a few medieval monuments and situated in a landscape of a fitfully stupefactive order. Fitfully, one must insist; for rarely are all the stops pulled out upon this organ; quite often the machinery clogs and the prodigious vision vanishes in a cloud of dust and steam. (Perhaps that is why a diorama is always available in the Alpineum to console those who have peered in vain through mist and fog.) In bad weather it is a good idea to explore the Jesuitenkirche (59), where the unvarying consolations of art may be enjoyed in all seasons. This church was built in 1666–73 by P. Christoph Vogler; a sister building to the Jesuitenkirche at Solothurn, it was inserted with all possible discretion into the medieval scheme of the city. Few buildings better reveal the good breeding of a true baroque exterior. Within, the stucco decoration of the choir and side-chapel are contemporary with the church itself; but the decorations of the

57 The Jungfrau above Wengen

59 Lucerne : the Jesuitenkirche (1666-73).
Architect, P. C. Vogler

58 Sarnen : the Pfarrkirche (1739-42).
Architects, Franz and J. A. Singer

nave—stucco, ceiling-paintings, altar-picture—date from 1749 to 1750, and most lightly and brilliantly do they offset the architect's monumental line.

There is one other fine church which celebrates with signal opulence the joy and fervour with which Lucerne accepted the rôle of leader in the struggle of the Catholic Cantons against the Reformation. Originally at the extreme edge of the town, the twin-spired Hofkirche is now one of its most central monuments. The two towers which rise with such breathtaking lightness at the top of the staircase were built in 1506 and 1515. After a fire had destroyed the rest of the original church in March 1633, a Jesuit, Jakob Khurer from Ingolstadt, devised the present building, which incorporates the two towers and their spires—"toothpick steeples", Mark Twain called them—in a conception of singular majesty.

There are of course many classical excursions from Lucerne; and of these the tour of the lake must be accounted the finest. Even those least susceptible to landscape of this kind must yield to its unforced grandeur. The lake is best seen by steamer. On a fine day, with nothing but the cough of the paddles to break into the silence, the journey will astound throughout its length, for Nature has planned her effects with the spatial assurance of the great Venetian masters. Myself afflicted with a bad memory for sublimities, I shall not venture to describe the tour in detail. The overland route is less satisfactory. Not only is there no continuous circular road (a mercy, in view of what has happened to other lakes), but so heavy is the traffic in good weather that it is impossible to enjoy the great theatrical strokes at leisure. The Axenstrasse must be considered a particularly hazardous stretch, from this point of view; nothing can really compare with the lumbering motion of the paddle-steamer, as the heavenly panorama shifts gradually into one's field of vision and the slap-slap of fresh water answers to the turning wheel. The unhurried poetry of such a progress can best offset the magnificence of the scene. (It is a good plan to take a book, all the same, in case it rains.)

On the very last leg of the circuit Tribschen comes into view on the left. A screen of poplars hides the three-storeyed cube; since the municipality of Lucerne acquired it in 1933, Wagner's villa has been kept in exemplary trim. An avenue of maples leads from the road to the garden gate, and the loose gravel before the perron is always freshly raked. A hole has been cut in the hedge to allow of a prospect through to the many-spired *bassin* of Lucerne, and the interior of the house has been filled with authentic and curious relics. There is Wagner's velvet beret; his house-jacket, his old Erard, his armchair;

his manuscripts, concert programmes, and the portraits of his friends and admirers; and some very perishable interpretations, in oil and water-colour, of favourite scenes from the operas. Nietzsche, Bülow, Houston Stewart Chamberlain, Liszt and Schopenhauer are here by right; so are the *inspiratrices*, the favourite singers and the bizarre trophies contributed by later enthusiasts. Is there something lacking? Are the lutes and the theorbos out of place on the first floor? The portraits, so surprising at a first glance, of Judith Gautier, Catulle Mendès and Villiers de L'Isle Adam suggest an answer, for Judith Gautier devoted the third volume of her memoirs to the story of her veneration for Wagner; and the most vivid of her pages are those which describe how, in 1869, these three French pilgrims paid their respects at Tribschen. Judith Gautier was nineteen at the time, and nothing could exceed her ingenuous raptures. Mendès, her husband, hardly appears in the book. The more febrile Villiers heartily seconded her frenzies, and hung avidly from the window of the train as it drew into what she called "the new Bethlehem". Wagner was on the platform to meet them. Boundless the courtesy of the exiled giant, and boundless the gratification of the distinguished Frogs! "Brusquely Villiers, white to the lips and with staring eyes, flung himself back into his seat, crying: "Tis he himself! The palm-bearer!""

Wagner was fond of the Lucerne hotels. It was at the Schweizerhof that he had completed *Tristan* in September 1859, and in the Hôtel du Lac, where he had taken rooms for his French admirers, he was later to rehearse that most princely of gifts, the *Siegfried Idyll*. From its balcony they watched him set off to prepare their welcome at Tribschen, walking across the Kapellbrücke and embarking upon the lake—"so pure, so clear," noted the diarist, "that it seemed an immense block of blue crystal, a liquid sapphire".

With the help of Judith Gautier's narrative one can re-infect the museum with something of Wagner's personality. In the master's study a contrived twilight softened the outline of the bookshelves, the piano (fitted with drawers) and the dark arras. The only picture in the room was a portrait of Ludwig II: the swarthy face, the penetrating polar-blue eyes. The scent of white roses clung even to the manuscript which lay open on the piano. The salon also was associated in Judith Gautier's mind with "a warm and reposeful penumbra". Purple damask and violet velvet made up the heavy, moth-inviting scheme of the room, while for preferred objects there were a row of Wagnerian heroes in white marble, some panels with scenes from the Nibelungenlied, a gilded Buddha, some chased goblets, Chinese incense-burners, and two round tables inlaid with azure and purple butterflies. The master himself was in variable mood. Now withdrawn, now boisterous as a boy of seven; now the hierophant, now the inventor of inconceivable puns. Once an ingrained love of the crescendo caused him to push Cosima von Bülow so violently upon the garden swing that the complaisant adulteress all but fell in a swoon; and once, while on a sight-seeing tour, he roused his guests at daybreak by singing the Marseillaise.

The unblemished idealism of this juvenile admirer is the best introduction to Tribschen. Those who examine, for example, Mr. Ernest Newman's definitive biography of Wagner will learn more, but they will not learn so agreeably; and when they close the book they will return more willingly to the score of *Meistersinger* than to the private history of its fallible creator. In this they will reverse the policy of the local authorities; for although these have taken great pains to restore many private tokens of Wagner's life in Lucerne, they rarely include his work in the programmes of their summer music-festival. These programmes have, on the whole, a prudential flavour which, though appropriate to Lucerne itself, may discourage an exacting listener. This is the more unfortunate as the acoustic of the concert-hall in the Kunsthaus is of a lustrousness hardly conceivable to Londoners, and allows the great inventions of Berlioz and Stravinsky to be given with ideal clarity; an unimaginable bloom returns to the surface of the Viennese repertory, and even Chopin's orchestration sounds like that of a master. It is the more disappointing, therefore, that no new works for large orchestra are commissioned, and that when Mr. Menuhin is so adventurous as to essay the concerto of Bartok, a vast middlebrow public should sit it out with unfeigned indifference.

*   *   *   *   *

Where landscape is concerned, it is always questionable policy to impose one's preferences upon others. For instance, the Lake of Zug is to me infinitely more congenial than the Lake of Como. I have few Swiss memories more happy than that of bathing in the warm waters of this disregarded and rather featureless mere. Barefoot among the apple orchards, or adrift upon the unbroken surface of the lake, I would not have exchanged my situation for any other in the world. One can be at the greatest pains to see as many monuments as the day will hold; and yet in the end the recurrent images of a past holiday may spring from quite a different source, and from a long summer in Switzerland one may remember best the face of a stranger glimpsed in a restaurant-car, a trolley full of wild flowers in a second-rate hotel, the delicate clicking of goats' feet upon stone, as the herds return home to Mesocco, or an enormous frog, motionless beside a stream on the Simplon. Why should one remember the frog (the sensitive apparatus of his mouth and nostrils, the firm, lucent jelly of his sides) when whole tracts of spectacular country have vanished for ever from the mind? I make this confession in order to warn my readers that this book is no substitute for Murray or Baedeker.

Ur-Schweiz comprises the cantons of Uri, Schwyz, Unterwalden and Lucerne; it includes the lakes of Lucerne, Zug, Sihl, Wäggital and Sempach; the towns of Lucerne, Zug, Schwyz, Sarnen, Andermatt, Altdorf, Fluelen and Stans; a part of the Klausen, Susten and Gotthard passes, and an unusual number of fine monuments of the Counter-Reformation, with Einsiedeln, Engelberg, St. Urban and Beromünster at their head. Although it includes, or is overlooked by, a great many high mountains, it is mostly made up of undulant agricultural country—orchard and pasture, with everywhere the sound of hurrying water. (In Altdorf, this persists even in the middle of the town, where grilles, let into the pavement, reveal fast-flying water a few inches below.) The fountains are never dry in the squares of Ur-Schweiz; often bowered in geraniums, they whisper quietly throughout the year, as they have whispered, in many cases, for five centuries. It rains a great deal in this country, until each roof becomes a chute of water and the countryside explores, ever more patiently, the possibilities of green. One must watch the lakes of Ur-Schweiz as they shudder and decompose beneath heavy rain; and afterwards one must pace the leafy quays and listen to the last drops of rain as they probe the foliage of chestnut and plane. One must know this country in July, when the sun strikes down on the terrace and sucks the colour from its awnings; when the midnight sky still shimmers with the heat of afternoon, and the wooden roofs painfully stretch and contract from hour to blazing hour. And one must come also in February, when snow gives place to grass (the colour of tobacco), and the Muota, the Seewen and the Sarneraa become torrents, milk-white and creamy, unimaginably rapid in their shallow beds. And at any season there are the huge white village-churches of Ur-Schweiz: not the masterpieces of European endeavour which I have just mentioned, but the big, blanched exteriors of the Pfarrkirche at Arth, or Lachen, or Gersau, or Schwyz (61); the rage for building which enriched Andermatt, for example, with three baroque churches or chapels in addition to the romanesque Church of St. Columba, itself done over at the same period. Not all these interiors are in the nicest taste; the innumerable paintings by Deschwanden, for example. . . . There is already, in many of these churches,

60 Zug : the Kirche
St. Oswald (*left*)

61 Schwyz : the
Pfarrkirche St. Mar-
tin (1769-74) (*right*)

62   Sarnen : the Square and the Fountain

63   Lucerne : the Rathaus

something of the savoury exuberance of the Ticinese chapels. Of course, there are fine churches of other periods; the Kirche St. Oswald at Zug (60), for instance, is perhaps the finest late Gothic parish church in Switzerland. First laid out in 1478, it assumed its present form at the end of the fifteenth century; the tower was added in 1557. The exterior of this church is also peculiarly rich in sculptures, both Gothic (*c.* 1500) and later. But such buildings are exceptional in Ur-Schweiz, and the typical landscape of these cantons will have in its foreground the plain white bulk of a seventeenth-century church, surmounted by its black or gold onion and standing perhaps a little above its village, in a plantation of saturated green. The tiny canton of Unterwalden is holy ground for those who enjoy such sights; and indeed all travellers should warm to it, for it includes, in undemonstrative fashion, some of the best country in Switzerland, and one of the most comforting legends. One may explore much of all this while motoring from Lucerne to Interlaken.

Unterwalden begins just after the little resort (an ideal base for those who wish to go to the Lucerne Festival, but not to stay in Lucerne) of Hergiswil. There comes a point at which the lake adjoins the smaller Alpnachersee, and the broad-beamed steamers may be seen crawling like landfish along the narrow canal which links the two. Already at Alpnach (in a landscape most refreshingly unassertive after the menacing grandeur of the Vierwaldstättersee) one may admire the church in the classical style built by Joseph Singer in 1812–20, and nearby, at Kerns, its sister building and exact contemporary, also by Singer. This versatile and energetic practitioner was one of a family which considerably embellished Ur-Schweiz between 1780 and 1820. Joseph Singer left his mark most copiously in Lucerne at the turn of the century; the Mint building in the Mühlenplatz, the interior of the Casino, the Sentispital, the orphanage in the Waisenstrasse, the Propstei or provost's house adjoining the Hofkirche, and the Albertis Haus near the Reussbrücke, would all seem to be by him; Louis XVI, Classic and Empire—all came easily to him, and at the end of his career he encompassed the Ionian splendours of the Empire church at Knutwil—not far from Triengen, where he had collaborated, a quarter of a century earlier, in a church of classical design.

Sarnen (62), four miles along the road from Alpnach, is one of the unimportant towns which make Switzerland memorable. Its main square has everything that is most agreeable; asymmetrical in plan, it is laid round a fountain, of which the basin, inscribed 1604, was adorned a century later with the statue of Nicholas of Flue. The almost maniacal cleanliness and civic pride of the Swiss have enabled the surrounding buildings to look as new as, or even newer than, the Hôtel Metzgern, which must be of the present century. Nothing imposes itself. The town hall, a building of considerable dignity (Sarnen, after all, is the Hauptstadt of the sub-canton of Obwald), was built in 1729–31 by Georg Urban, an architect with a good practice in Lucerne. Inside are the statutory features: the rococo decorations in the Ratsaal, the portraits of former worthies (oaken in their simplicity), and as a local speciality the portrait of Nicholas of Flue. The Rathaus at Sarnen is perfectly in character. It adjoins the square but does not dominate it. At most its quoins (redone a few years ago) and the shutters with their brilliant diagonal zigzags suggest that this is the lawful centre of the town. At the other end of the square the Dorfkapelle, the most recent of the five ecclesiastical buildings in Sarnen, has on the ground-floor the aspect of a celestial cricket-pavilion; above, whorls and pilasters, and the suggestion of a pedimented doorway opening into mid-air, complete this curious but most alluring façade. The other houses round the square are of many periods, but they bear an unchanging family face; no matter whether they are four hundred years old or were built yesterday, they live together in amity. Lettering, whether Roman or Gothic, does not disturb the rhythm of steep-pitched, long-eaved roofs (often descending more than half-way to the ground), shutters closed against the noonday sun, and between every house a glimpse of green beyond. To the north there stands upon an eminence the Schützenhaus. Built as an arsenal in 1752, this exquisite building is now as pacific as the rest of the landscape. It is one of many examples in Ur-Schweiz of the way in which white (if it be "furiously white", as Leibniz suggests) can be a positive force in landscape design. One cannot exaggerate the brilliance of this little fortress, with its elegant central block, armigerous and saddle-backed; its flanking, single-storeyed wings, each crowned with a cupola and black onion; and the dazzling zigzag of its shutters. Nor have I even begun to enumerate the ecclesiastical splendours of Sarnen. The Pfarrkirche involves us in further acquaintance with the great family of Singer, to whom this countryside owes so much of its beauty and interest. Itself dating from 1739 to 1742, it is the work of Franz and Johann Anton Singer. Franz Singer has no other church to his credit, but his colleague was responsible, either alone or in concert with Jakob Singer, for the redoubtable churches of Cham, Schwyz and Wolfenschiessen. Sarnen boasts also the Friedhofkapelle; this will delight those who, already permeated with the legend of Nicholas of Flue, may wish to see a relic of his period. Even Dr. Jenny, no complaisant critic, declared that it had "one of the loveliest late-Gothic carved and painted wood-ceilings in Switzerland". This was executed in 1505 by Peter von Uri, whose work appears in more dubious form in the Untere Ranftkapelle and the Musli-Kapelle at Flueli.

After so long a dalliance in the Ronuk-scented churches of Sarnen, it is a redoubled pleasure to re-encounter the peaceable landscape—the lakeside, spongy and pierced with reeds, the orchards so loaded with fruit that the heavier branches need a crutch to prevent them from snapping, and in the distance the roofs of Sarnen and the white radiance of a church. (Gonzague de Reynold has well likened these roofs to nutshells heaped, as if by a squirrel, beneath a mound of grass.) It is in this landscape that Nicholas von der Flue was born in 1417; and here he lived for fifty years, farming, taking his share in the management of the province, and raising a family of ten children. His wife, Dorothea Wyssling, was also from Sachseln. She had just borne him the tenth of their children when Nicholas decided, in 1467, to abandon the world and become a hermit. Though drawn, in his mind, towards some distant retreat in the Black Forest or the Vosges, he had walked no farther than to Liestal, near Berne, when the thought of his native scene began to exert upon him its old, inexpugnable power. Back he came; and for his hermitage he chose a place on the Ranft, not far from Sachseln. There he lived for twenty years, and schooled himself to go altogether without food or drink. Even the Bishop of Constance was forced to concede that this was something out of the way; and when other miracles were added to it, the renown of Bruder Klaus, as he was popularly called, began to attract an ever greater number of pilgrims. The lonely, the penitent and the curious were welcomed impartially, until the effort of receiving them, and of attending to their importunities, seemed likely to curtail the life of the anchorite. Intermediaries were then appointed, and Bruder Klaus was able to amble unmolested in the meadow before his cell. Those who were allowed to see him in audience reported that, though unable to read or to write, he knew long passages from the Scriptures by heart, and that often he answered their questions even before they had put them to him. It also got about that he made an annual appearance at Einsiedeln without ever having been seen on the road in either direction.

All this is singular enough; but singularity alone would not explain the veneration in which Nicholas von der Flue is still held throughout Switzerland. It would not account, for instance, for the crowds which throng the church at Sachseln in which the hermit is buried. The black marble of Melchtal has been used copiously in the church, which dates from 1672 to 1684, and pilgrims have to edge their way forward through a forest of jet. What brings them there? Not, one would suppose, the personal beauty of Bruder Klaus; for all portraits of him agree upon the woefully bent and emaciated figure, the drooping and striated countenance of the holy counsellor. People come because Nicholas von der Flue is the symbol of peace and conciliation, and because he exemplified—inaugurated, indeed—the policy of watchful conciliation which Switzerland has followed, though with ever greater difficulty, during the period which has laid her neighbours in ruins. For that reason the church at Sachseln and the hill-country above it are at present the most intensely venerated of all Swiss shrines. For most English tourists, the peace, security and outward opulence of Swiss life are an axiom, a fact as immutable as the height of Everest; to the Swiss, on the contrary, they are perishable possessions—long fought for, often in jeopardy, much coveted by others and needing to be kept in perfect repair.

After an early morning visit to Sachseln, many possibilities lie open to the enquiring traveller. He can visit Engelberg, for instance, and on the way he can call at Stans (64), the scene of Bruder Klaus's final intervention in 1481. This is a beautiful small town; a timely conflagration (in 1713) gave the signal for the construction, in the following year, of many of the elegantly gabled buildings which now adorn the Dorfplatz and the Rathausplatz, and in 1791 Nikolaus Purtschert, the architect of the classical churches at Buochs and Beckenried, built the Breitenhaus, in which he has emulated the Louis XVI style with all the agility of his great contemporaries, the Singers.

Beyond Stans the road runs through the exemplary orchards of Nidwalden; it is difficult to associate the unpretending beauties of this landscape with the heroic action by which, in September 1798, the men of the Niderwald refused to swear allegiance to their French masters and courageously resisted the armies of Schauenburg. In their own green-shadowed country the little force held out as best they could; but the French armies were too strong, and they exacted a fearful vengeance. More than seven hundred houses were burnt down and nearly four hundred people, many of them women and children, were massacred. We continue alongside the fast-flowing and milky Engelbergeraa, and past Wolfenschiessen, where one should pause to admire J. A. Singer's Pfarrkirche (1775–7), which was erected on the site of its medieval predecessor. Bruder Scheuber, the son-in-law of Bruder Klaus, and himself a hermit, is buried at Wolfenschiessen, and near the church one may see the wooden blockhouse in which he lived; this was moved down, after his death, from Bettelruti, beneath the Wellenberg. Then the road narrows,

64   Stans : the Convent of St. Klara (1627)

65 The Eiger, Mönch and Jungfrau

and one begins the long, leafy climb to Engelberg. At Grafenort, there comes the first outpost of the Abbey—the Heiligkreuzkapelle, built in 1689 and attached to a country house of quality. Soon afterwards one sights the spectacular cascades of the Aa, and after a considerable pull the Abbey itself, and the town of Engelberg, come into view.

Engelberg, like Stans, knew when to go up in smoke; after the great fire of 1729 the present buildings were erected between 1730–37. As often happened, the commission was given to an architect from the Vorarlberg, Johannes Rueff, who later worked at Einsiedeln and at the Benedictine Abbey at Fischingen. There is a certain splendid plainness, not to say dullness, about his grandiose creation, which is more imposing at a distance or from the heights towards the Trübsee, than on close examination. Engelberg itself is a charmless little town, redeemed only by certain Edwardian survivals—the well-upholstered fiacres, the art-nouveau tea-rooms, and the solid, slightly derelict façade of the main streets. Henry James confided to one of his notebooks an opinion of this high-lying plateau which is still valid, half a century later: "The Engelberg, that grim, ragged, rather vacuous, but by no means absolutely unbeautiful valley." It is pleasant to be slung up in a cage to the Trübsee, though this little lake has been well and thoroughly tamed, and the rock-landscape which faces one is of a confined and rather hideous sort. The excursion exemplifies, indeed, the aspects of Swiss tourism which make fastidious people stay at home. Nothing is here for private delight; unless, that is to say, we climb high up, towards the coated tongue of the glacier, and there, with a torrent to cool the air, spread out a collation of eggs, ham, white wine and peaches.

Suppose, however, that instead of visiting Stans and Engelberg we have gone straight on, past Sachseln, past the diminutive Lungernsee, past the wooden village of Lungern, up and up and up to the top of the Brünig Pass. The countryside has the yielding, palpable sweetness of central Switzerland; and the Lungernsee, though generally not much esteemed, drew a discerning tribute from at any rate one early Victorian tourist—John Hogg, who acclaimed "that bijou—the small but most enchanting of lakes, the Lake of Lungern, of which the water is an exquisite blue, transparent and truly 'splendidior vitro' ". The Brünig Pass is not really very high for Switzerland: only 3,400 feet; but it differs from the other greater passes in being densely wooded, so that one's progress is through an upward tunnel of boskage; green calls to green until, at the summit of the pass, one is made free of a great stretch of new country. Among other things, the Faulhorn, the Engelhörner, the Aar Valley and the falls of Oltschibach and Reichenbach. Admirers of Sherlock Holmes will crane eagerly towards the last of these features; others, once at the bottom of the easy and wide-ranging *lacets* which make up the other half of the pass, may seek advice as to where to go next. Meiringen will not detain them, for there the conflagration was very badly timed. Eighteen-ninety-one was not a good year for architecture anywhere in the world, and Meiringen is not a thing of beauty to-day. As if to balance this fate, however, the town can boast the oldest-dated clock in the cantons of Bern; this adorns the detached Romanesque tower of the local church. From Meiringen one can strike west, along the flat delta of the Aar, to Brienz and the Brienzersee. This lake, with its steep and wooded northern shore, has an intimate pathos not lost upon travellers who, like Byron and Goethe before them, put up at Brienz. The town itself is little more than a vast manufactory of wooden souvenirs; if, however, one drives on to Interlaken, one finds there what is virtually an Edwardian spa, laid out with public parks in the English style (one looks instinctively for the pavilion, the sight-screen and the scoreboard); only in the walnut-shaded Höheweg does it step out of character, for there one may gaze upon the un-English spectacle of Jungfrau, Mönch and Eiger (65). I cannot pretend that Interlaken itself is very stirring; but from it one may visit such gratifying phenomena as the Staubbach, the Trümmelbach Falls, the Upper Fall of the Schmadribach, and the glaciers of Grindelwald. The enjoyments need no word from me. Let one of the greatest of Alpinists speak in my place. "The Oberland wall", F. S. Smythe wrote, "is unique; there is nothing like it in the world. There is the mighty lift of the Himalayas from the Indian plains, the icy savagery and remoteness of the mountains of Yukon and Alaska, and the southern fall of Mont Blanc . . . yet in the memories and affections of all who know it there is nothing quite like the Oberland." Once these magnificences have been savoured, the tourist will soon weary of the Bödeli (the enervating alluvial junction upon which Interlaken rests) and will dart either towards Thun, and thus out of this chapter, or back towards Meiringen, in which case he can set off, in the summer months, for the adventure of the Susten Pass.

Alpine passes are no longer among the symbolic ordeals of human existence, but the Susten Pass is at least still new; and the road itself, superbly metalled and furnished with every convenience for the toiling motorist, uncoils itself among scenery of prehistoric grandeur, and as the orchards drop away above Innertkirchen and the carriage-way passes through buttress after buttress of projecting rock, the landscape assumes an authentic desolation. We cannot now hope to emulate the Englishman who, in 1775, was the first person to cross the Gotthard in a wheeled carriage; but as we attack the Susten we can still sense that few people have been here before; even the bridle-path was first made in the Napoleonic era. The country is lunar in aspect, and traversed only by foaming torrents; in the narrow valley the sun burns one *lacet* to a Spanish dryness, leaving the other cold and oozy with damp. Even the summit of the Susten, though defaced by a car-park and several booths of primitive refreshment, is still a memorable *Blick*. One gazes on the white bowler of the Gwächtenhorn; the wind blows cool from the glacier, which lies, like the tongue of a dead lion, beneath our platform; and in the great waste of dead matter which lies below and around, one cannot but admire the delicate, humanizing curves of the white-posted road as it gleams blue and grey in the sunshine. (No less beautiful is the Euclidean statement of the Grimsel barrage, with the Finsteraarhorn behind, and the buttress of the artificial lake whorled like a conch.)

The eastern half of the Susten Pass is, if anything, almost more desolate and arresting than the western, for the long, sloping trough of the Meiental offers many parching perspectives of unflowering rock. Even when the Pass has been completed and we turn right at Göschenen in order to make for Andermatt, a further ordeal is in store; for the Reuss, last seen in peaceable though impetuous form at Lucerne, here enters a granite canyon of claustrophobic character. The journey is thus one in which there is really no relief from the Mappin Terrace style of landscape; nor, I must own, does Andermatt proffer many rewards to the more sedentary type of tourist. Though scenically more advantageous, it is at bottom a sort of Swiss Didcot—a junction, that is to say, for the four great roads which converge upon it. It is also, for the same reason, a great military centre. D. H. Lawrence found it "terribly raw and flat and accidental", and there is no need to controvert him; even the great alpinists, after all, chafe and fret if the weather compels them to pass a whole day in such towns. There are better places in which to take leave of the four cantons; let us complete the tour of Ur-Schweiz with more northerly pleasures.

The Klausen Pass, for instance. From Altdorf to the top of the pass, this presents a scene of classical desolation. The road, moreover, is by no means new, so that motorists may be able, often involuntarily, to duplicate the *frissons* of Horace Walpole and Gray, as a crumbling surface (or an encounter with another vehicle) leads them towards the abyss. In its upmost reaches the Klausen road winds among rude stone hutches, with the tinkle of cow-bells ever audible from the rich pasturage of Urnerboden. This curious valley which can boast a very comfortable hotel, lies at 4,000 feet; it is agreeable to rise early at Urnerboden, while the sun can hardly abate the vivifying cold, and to mount the grassy slopes. It is a mistake, however, to climb the minor eminences which abound on the pasture, since these are generally topped with a carpet of goat-droppings. Beyond the valley, one may enjoy one of those splendid contrasts of temper and expression in which Art is so often more successful than Nature. Here, at least, there is no flaw; and the ruined height of the Klausen gives place to a landscape of Elysian green. The Fätschbach, which earlier has watered the valley of Urnerboden, here tumbles down to the valley in which the Linth races along its stony bed; and as we pursue our more decorous course, we hear everywhere— above, around, below—the murmuration of numberless trees, and the sun, now nearly overhead, is filtered and refracted by overhanging leaves.

It would be an excess of courtesy to pretend that most English visitors to Switzerland are well read in Swiss history. We no more think of studying the Burgundian era than a Brazilian visitor to Ascot would think of studying the Wars of the Roses. For those, however, who enjoy the great Alpine passes there is a particular interest in the Napoleonic era. It was Napoleon who ordered the construction of the Simplon Pass in 1800, soon after the Battle of Marengo; and after Napoleon himself had fallen, and the perpetual neutrality of Switzerland had been guaranteed at the Congress of Vienna, other great ventures were undertaken—among them the St. Gotthard, Splügen and San Bernardino Passes. Moreover, the battles of 1799, though crippling in their effect upon the Swiss countryside, afford some fantastic examples of human endurance. The armies of General Suvorow, for instance, crossed the high Alps four times in fourteen days. "I believe", wrote William Wickham, "there is no example of a march that can be compared to this in the history of the world." Wickham, who had married a Swiss and was devoted to her country, was sent on a special mission to the Allied Armies by Lord Grenville, the British Foreign Secretary; his despatches, published in 1870, give a lurid and precise account of the inefficiency, the in- decision and the mutual lack of confidence among the Allies which finally forced Suvorow to execute these prodigies of valour. Between June and September Masséna, the French C.-in-C., was able to recover entirely the advantage which he had lost by the first battle of Zürich (after which he had had to retire to the Limmat, the Reuss and the Aare), and on September 25th he routed the Allies, now represented by Russia in place of Austria, at the second battle of Zürich. In advancing from the line of the Aare he had fought many a skirmish on the Susten and Grimsel Passes; but his journey was a pleasure-party compared with that of Suvorow. At the time of the second battle of Zürich (during which the Russian troops were often heard to call upon the name of Suvorow, in the hope that he would arrive in time to tip the scale), Suvorow himself had just reached Andermatt after fighting his way over the Gotthard. A passage of any kind was exhausting and hazardous in those days, but Suvorow had had to engage the French forces repeatedly, from the gorges of Stalvedro (below Airolo) right up to the last stages of the pass; and there they dealt a final blow by destroying a great part of the Devil's Bridge, which alone affords a passage over the ravine of the Reuss. Suvorow himself has described the awful scenes which followed: the rough substitute, built of planks tied together with officers' sashes, which constantly gave way and plunged both men and horses into the foaming abyss. Small wonder that, when they reached Andermatt, the Russians were so hungry that for lack of better victuals they ate soap and leather by the ton. They made on down the valley of the Reuss towards Zürich, but were halted at Altdorf; there being at that time no Axenstrasse, the panoramic splendours of the Vierwaldstättersee presented an impassable barrier to an invading army. Suvorow therefore made a detour and crossed the Kinzig-Kulm (6,792 feet); after this his men were in understandably poor shape for fighting, and they failed to carry the entrance to the Muotatal. In despair he turned to the east, marched his men over the Pragel Pass to Glarus, and thence in the first week of October, by way of the snow-covered Panixer (7,897 feet), to winter-quarters in the Grisons and Austria.

One cannot read of such feats without curiosity as to the man who directed them. Suvorow was an unorthodox soldier. Devoted to English beer and English forthrightness ("*C'est un vrai God Damn!*" he exclaimed on reading Wickham's first despatch), he by no means followed English custom in the direction of affairs. Openly disdainful of his officers, he allowed his men to loot and plunder as they pleased, in the belief that they would yield the more readily when he called for a supreme effort. Wickham was disposed to think this immoral in principle but sound in practice. "The elements of which the Russian troops are composed", he wrote, "are such that, when put together, they cannot be called an *army* in any respect but the number of men." Long years of service had persuaded Suvorow that it was quite hopeless to undertake the tactics which his soldierly intuition would naturally suggest to him. Consequently his behaviour was governed by an ironical foreboding of disappointment. Wickham breakfasted with him on October 13th, 1799; so far from betraying fatigue or distress at the turn of events, he turned the occasion into a carnival, walking about the room "with his hands and his head hanging like those of an idiot; talking nonsense to everybody, mixed occasionally with shrewd and sensible remarks on all kinds of subjects. The dinner, the whole manner of serving it, and above all the servants who attended, were so very dirty and disgusting that General Jellachich, though a Croat, could not bring himself to eat a single mouthful, at which the Marshal either was, or affected to be, much offended. After the meal, which lasted three hours, he went immediately to bed, and did not get up till four, nor see anybody till five in the afternoon; and it is in this manner that the best part of the day is constantly lost." Suvorow knew his men too well to demand from them anything more; to all Wickham's entreaties he returned a Roman insistence upon the value of comfortable winter-quarters; and so he passes out of the history of Switzerland.

Later, larger and even more futile campaigns have pushed the battles of 1799 down into the footnotes of history. Even the landscape has forgotten them; the burned houses of Altdorf have been rebuilt, and of the depredations of the rival armies there is no longer any trace. And if there lingers, in any family of Ur-Schweiz, a mysterious Russian strain, the passing motorist will have to look very hard to find it. We are as healthily indifferent to the sufferings of our forbears as our descendants will be to our own. Nature's upheavals are more lasting, as we may judge from the great boulders which litter the road east of Arth-Goldau. These were dislodged when the Rossberg collapsed in 1806; mournful trophies of this great landslide may still be seen by anyone who takes the road from Lucerne to Einsiedeln.

Einsiedeln! I have kept this great treat until last. Loath to leave Ur-Schweiz upon any but a joyous note, I wished to preserve for my readers, not a retreat of Suvorovian character towards winter-quarters in London, but an excursion into the amiable uplands which conceal this peerless monument. Peerless, that is to say, in our present experience; for while there is no doubt that examples as good or better may exist in Austria or South Germany, I consider Einsiedeln to be, with St. Gall, the most exhilarating edifice in the whole of Switzerland. In itself it would repay the journey from England.

One can reach Einsiedeln as easily from Zürich as from Lucerne, but I do not recommend this route. The road along the Zürichsee is of unsurpassed banality, whereas its rival winds among unfrequented country of great beauty. There is the Lake of Zug; Arth and Goldau are small towns of quality; and a detour will take us to Schwyz, where Jakob and Johann Anton Singer built, in 1769–74, a parish church only equalled for majesty by that at Lachen, at the eastern end of the Zürichsee. Schwyz (61) is the town from which all Switzerland derives its name, and it contains an unusual number of good early seventeenth-century buildings; Swiss bourgeois architecture of the late Renaissance and early Baroque periods can be studied as profitably in Schwyz as anywhere. Do not fail, therefore, to seek out the Ital' Reding'sches Haus, hideous as this is, the Rathaus, the Haus Kundig and the Palais von Weber. But go back in good time to climb the valley of the Steiner-Aa; by the time Rothenturm is reached, the air has become cool and the wind blows fresh and brisk. This is a high plateau, at nearly 3,000 feet, upon which peat is cut and an ancient puffer stands coughing at the cutters' elbow. This aged locomotive, stationary in the pine-bordered and soggy plain, gives the signal that Einsiedeln is at hand. After Biberbrücke the road runs through the forest, with an aromatic saw-mill to point the way. The great building does not raise itself, like Chartres, vertical in a horizontal world; it may once have done so, for it stands at the top of a shallow hill, but in the last century a town of miscellaneous ugliness has pushed itself up to the Klosterplatz—perhaps to cater for the "crowd of palmers and votaries" whom Gibbon saw "prostrate before the altar" when, at the age of eighteen, he visited the abbey. "I was astonished", he recalled many years later, "by the profuse ostentation of riches in the poorest corner of Europe; amidst a savage scene of woods and mountains, a palace appears to have been erected by magic; and it was erected by the potent magic of religion."

Gibbon went there in 1755, when the magic was very recent; after two centuries a curious collection of architectural rubbish has come to obscure the original effect of the abbey, much as the Arcadian beaches of the Ægean are sometimes littered with filth by a passing liner. Gibbon appreciated the abbey, but his enjoyment was disturbed by a scruple which is unlikely to distress the pilgrims of our own day. "The title and worship of the Mother of God", he wrote, "provoked my indignation; and the lively naked image of superstition suggested to me, as in the same place it had done to Zwingli, the most pressing argument for the reformation of the church." My readers will surely not be so nice; for, although it is easy to mistake indifference for tolerance, I cannot think that any English visitor would be so churlish as not to emulate the perfect discretion with which the Swiss now leave every citizen free to worship what, and how, he pleases.

Einsiedeln has never, to my knowledge, been adequately described in English. Gibbon's unpublished journal of his first Swiss tour has excellent passages, but the great building itself does not emerge. Later travellers are for the most part openly disdainful; and one guide-book, in many ways the best of those available, says only that the abbey, "rebuilt in the modern Italian style (1704–70) is remarkable for its size and situation rather than its architecture". It was visited in the 1830s by that practised topographer and social observer H. D. Inglis. He was pleased, even astonished, by the buildings, but did not venture to describe them. Affluent pilgrims, many of them with their own carriages, then gave Einsiedeln the aspect "of a great fair, and the most novel perhaps, in its general features, of any to be seen in Europe". The women especially held his attention; nor can one be surprised, since some of them wore "the ancient bodkin, shaped like a dart, passing through the hair, with the head in the form of a diamond, and studded with glittering stones; others had a coiffure of plaited and stiffened lace, placed flat upon the head, upright like a cock's comb, or a large fan. Some had a broad circular piece of straw, placed flat upon the head, with flowers disposed tastefully in the centre. . . . Almost all the old women", he concludes, "carried staffs; and most of the young, red umbrellas." To-day's pilgrims will not leave us comparably agog, but they are sufficiently numerous to give Einsiedeln the animation which its scenic planning so winningly invites.

The Benedictine Abbey of Einsiedeln is just over a thousand years old. It was founded in 934 by Domherr Benno from Strasburg, upon the site of the cell inhabited in the ninth century by Meinrad, a hermit. The present building (66) is the sixth to occupy the site; of the others, the second, which was built between 1031–9 at the time when the remains of Meinrad were brought from Reichenau to Einsiedeln, the fourth (built between 1415 and 1510 by Hans Niesenberger, the architect of much of the minster at Freiburg-im-Breisgau), and the fifth, which appears in Meryan's engraving of the abbey, must be esteemed important; but it is improbable that any of them can have rivalled the abbey as we see it to-day. The exterior is in no wise extravagant. Baroque planning of this sort relies less on the profusion than on the perfect spacing of its effects; and, besides, Einsiedeln is not an ornamental building. It is not primarily a palace, but a self-sufficing settlement, in which room had to be found for kitchens, dormitories, a library, a bookbinding shop, a hospital, a laundry, a printing press, a bakery, a fire-station and a market-garden. Many kinds of people live at Einsiedeln, and the charity of Baroque is extended to them all. Abbot and ironmaster, glazier and acolyte, schoolmaster and boilerman—all are housed in one huge establishment. Admittedly many of them are lodged to one side, in

66　The Benedictine Abbey of Einsiedeln

67   Einsiedeln : Angel above the Choir (*sculptor, J. B. Babel*)

the long pavilions which German historians so bluntly distinguish as the Economy-Tract; but even these have a simple dignity which no other age has been able to better.

The main block of Einsiedeln forms a hollow square, of which the middle is divided into four large gardens by the vast cross-shaped buildings which comprise the abbey church and its dependencies. The west front of the block is not sumptuous but, as I have implied, it achieves an effect of great magnificence. Baroque planning is in large degree the art of making empty spaces count; and whereas the great Gothic cathedrals of Europe can rarely be seen to full advantage, so encumbered are they with irrelevant neighbours, the churches of Einsiedeln and St. Gall are set off by spatial planning of the greatest nicety. The general plans of the new abbey were executed between 1704 and 1770; they had been devised by Caspar Moosbrugger, who had been a lay brother of the abbey since 1681; after he had died in 1723, Brother Thomas Meyer took over the direction of the work for ten years. Johann Moosbrugger, brother of Caspar, and (from 1746 onwards) Joseph Rueff, the builder of Engelberg, were in charge of many of the later operations. When Moosbrugger first got out his plans, he had practically a free hand; the only parts of the present abbey then standing were the outline of the choir, and the little confessional-chapel which leads off to the north, and leads in its turn to the Magdalenenkapelle. These had been erected during Moosbrugger's time as a lay-brother (and perhaps with his help) by Hans Jörg Kuen who, like the Moosbruggers, was from the Bregenz area. There was also the Gnadenkapelle, in which was preserved the famous Black Madonna of Einsiedeln, and the Fountain of the Virgin which stands about a hundred yards in front of the main entrance to the church. This fountain (also from Kuen's hand) is now the westward limit of a design which has been allowed to work itself out, with the organic, inevitable rhythms of a work of art, over a space of more than three hundred yards, until it reaches the counterpart of the Liebfraubrunnen—the little fountain which plays among the lime-avenues at the east end of the abbey.

The Klosterplatz was laid out, in its present form, in 1748–9. It is essentially a simple though cunning device for heightening the effect of the shallow incline which leads to the abbey. One need not be an authority on style to sense how the eye is gathered in by the semicircular arcades and swept through the gap, up the staircase and on to the façade of the church, where the architects have allowed themselves a certain elaboration and brilliance of detail in order to contain and satisfy our excitement. There is nothing particular in this, or in the skill with which the arcades, though vital to the general effect, never obtrude upon the main building. There is conscious art in the way in which, where everything else (even the flanking garden-walls) yields to the eye in a series of recessed curves, the entrance to the church bends suddenly outwards, and towards us, as if swollen by the splendours within. Yet these are the pleasures of geometry only— the few, telling horizontals of the staircase, and the sudden convergence of upward and downward lines upon the gap in the arcades. They would seem insufficient for so large a space if it were not for a factor which Moosbrugger can hardly have foreseen—the great gifts of Johann Baptist Babel. Babel came to Einsiedeln in 1746, when he was thirty-one, and worked there till his death in 1798. He is thought to have been a native of Augsburg. His statues on the Klosterplatz must have been his first large commission at Einsiedeln, and they embellish the west front of the abbey with something of the lavish humanity which we shall find in superabundance within the church. The Emperors Otto I and Heinrich II dominate the steps with a grandeur that is never tyrannical, and a conversational stance which Babel has extended even to Benno, the founder of the abbey, as he stands above the garden gateway on the extreme right of the façade. Babel had before him the six statues executed for the façade of the church itself, in 1730, by Franz Antoni Kuen; flanked by the two slender towers, these now take up the reassuring message of Babel's emperors. I hesitate to elucidate this, for there can be no greater impertinence than to presume to analyse the aspirations of a foreign people; but these churches are so unlike our own that I must make the attempt. The notions of terror and dread, so familiar in more northerly churches, have very little place at Einsiedeln. The explosive world of the Old Testament, compact of unnatural crimes, unaccountable vengeances and insoluble family feuds, has been packed off to the archive-room. Nor have all the more terrible aspects of the New Testament been commemorated here; even Mary Magdalen at the foot of the Cross has been turned (or so one historian asserts) into a rococo idyll.

The image of Einsiedeln, to one pilgrim at least, is not that of the suffering, guilt-laden humanity invoked by the great Gothic cathedrals, but rather of a humanity perfected by the love of God and subject to rulers, both sacred and temporal, in whom the power to punish and torment is always tempered by reason and justice. The abbey church is itself, as we shall see when we push open the door, one of the most harmonious acts of adoration to which the eighteenth century attained.

Everything was in its favour. Even the Etzel sandstone, of which so much of it is built, could be quarried near at hand and has weathered beautifully. Add to this a succession of wise abbots, a team of first-rate creative craftsmen, and above all a generation in which everyone —architect, builder, sculptor and painter—spoke the same eloquent, flexible and infinitely suggestible language. One could not even conceive of a similarly successful church being built to-day; as for the League of Nations building—in some ways the secular counterpart of this abbey—I need only mention its name to bring before the reader a chaos of futile expenditure.

Moosbrugger had to incorporate in his new church the Gnaden-kapelle, which had been built on the site of Meinrad's cell by Santias Solari, the builder of Salzburg Cathedral. This chapel was pillaged by the French armies in 1798, but the present substitute leans heavily upon Solari's imposing black marble design; one cannot think that it was a good plan either to add, in 1821, the insignificant statues on the cornice, or to gild the Corinthian capitals, as was done in 1911. The interior of the chapel (68) is of course dominated by the figure of the Black Madonna. The image itself is a wooden statue of the fifteenth century, dressed with real magnificence, crowned and sceptred, laid against a brilliant golden aureole and surrounded by gold and silver hearts, the gift of earlier pilgrims. Restrained Ionic pilasters alone embroider the lustrous midnight of her marble surround. She is a memorable figure, and Moosbrugger must have wondered how best to set off her black tabernacle. Finally he devised a domed octagon of breathtaking richness. This style of architecture is sometimes reproached for its lack of mystery, and of course it is not easy to be mysterious in white and gold; nor do the round arch, the painted ceiling, the stuccoed columns and the enchainments of angels invoke the sense of loneliness and insufficiency which is part of the lesson of Gothic. Stained glass darkens all but a part of Bourges or Chartres, and infuses that part with an unearthly radiance quite unknown in baroque churches; earthly splendours alone have garnished Einsiedeln, although it would be foolish to infer from this that the spiritual history of this community is less noble or intense than that of the most unbending of Gothic foundations. The baroque artist has in some respects a harder task than the Gothic. His idiom can so easily become insipid, bloated or perfunctory. Indeed, we know that it did become so, and as we follow the history of this sixth abbey church we cannot but throw some anxious glances at the clock. Sixty-six years are a long time in the history of art; they measure the gap between Sir John Soane and Sir Gilbert Scott, or between Charlotte Brontë and Mr. Norman Douglas, or between Richard Wilson and J. M. W. Turner. Consider, again, the probable aspect of an abbey, first laid out in 1884 and due for completion in 1950.

The creators of Einsiedeln worked on the edges of chaos, but they never stepped over; and if, on our tour, we detect small flaws of taste or execution, they will almost certainly relate to the amendments of the last hundred and fifty years. (The gigantic chandelier given by Napoleon III, for example, is more suited to a Levantine bazaar.)

The structure of the octagon was finished in 1724, and work was at once begun on the two smaller domes, the Abendmahlskuppel and the Weihnachtskuppel, which lead towards the choir. At the same time the brothers Asam, then in their thirties and already famous for their work in southern German churches, came to Einsiedeln and remained for two years. Much of the beauty of the church derives from them, for Kosmas Damian Asam painted, with his usual untiring and monumental fluency, the frescoes upon all three of the available great expanses of ceiling, while Egid Quirin Asam lavished his plasterer's art with regal impartiality upon all the flat surfaces which Moosbrugger had provided. Capitals, cartouches, reliefs, *putti*, flying angels and allegorical groups poured forth inexhaustibly from the mind and hand of E. Q. Asam. Unlike some of his successors, he always respected the overriding importance of Moosbrugger's outlines; for in these, and in the endless resonances of white and gold, the calling and answering of one perspective to another, and the mutual thrusting and yielding between one arch, one dome, one gallery and its peers—in these relations, rather than in mere multiplication of grandeurs, does the genius of baroque reside. The art of the Asams is of a scrupulous but full-hearted sort. The two Bavarians were never abstract or intellectual in their approach; they were copious, sanguine and disinhibited workmen, who spoke in direct, bodily terms of what they most enjoyed; and during their two years at Einsiedeln they perpetuated their robust and appreciative outlook in vista upon vista of compositions in which painting and decoration spoke the same language.

Einsiedeln at that period was a rendezvous for artists and craftsmen of every kind. In all 317 men were employed in building the abbey, and the records would suggest that there reigned among them that strict but genial comradeship which we hopefully impute to the collective ventures of the Middle Ages. The work was hard. When Abbot Maurus von Roll ceremoniously launched the great enterprise, in March 1704, he did so at five o'clock in the morning; but later the hours were from four in the morning until seven in the evening; three times each summer, however, this discipline was relaxed, and great banquets were given to the artists and craftsmen who were labouring in wood and in stone, in plaster and in marble, in silver and in gold, to make this church as we know it—a terrestrial paradise.

As we approach the choir, new artists and new materials come into view. Hitherto (if we discount for a moment the side-chapels) the infinitely pliable art of the Asams has kept us in a trance of pleasure; baroque is an art of motion, above all things, and the nave of Einsiedeln contains few points of rest for the eye; there is instead a continuous, celestial hallooing of motives from floor to ceiling—and often too, a plunge into those unexpected, jewelled tunnels which Moosbrugger has devised for the visitors' astonishment. The choir-gate, which was built in the abbey workshops in 1675–85 and designed by Br. Vinzenz Nussbaumer, is of wrought-iron; the designer has so foreshortened the perspective of the three great doors that one has the illusion of looking down a *tonnelle*, an elegant piece of garden furniture, towards the Hochaltar (68). In the altar itself we come for the first time under direct Italian influence. Moosbrugger and the Asams are Bavarians—more inclined, that is, to lyrical than to dramatic statement. The confrontation of opposites is, on the other hand, the essence of Italian style; Nature has set, after all, a cracking pace in those latitudes, whereas in South Germany and the Tyrol sensuous, rather than passionate counsels prevail. The Hochaltar was sketched out by Gian Antonio Torricelli and executed by Domenico Pozzi, who also made the statue of the Virgin which now stands in the Liebfraubrunnen, in front of the church. In itself, the Hochaltar is a worthy point of focus. The repeated soaring columns are handicapped, however, by the very indifferent and deplorably extensive painting which Deschwanden was allowed, in 1880, to substitute for Franz Kraus's original. Kraus was responsible for the building of the choir, in 1746, on the site of the one designed seventy years earlier by H. G. Kuen. He was from Augsburg, and he spent the last six years of his life at Einsiedeln. Like most of his colleagues, he enjoyed a full life, rather than a long one, and his mark can be found in many parts of the abbey. One may judge, moreover, from his altar-painting in the Oberchor that it would have been a better plan to leave the Hochaltar as he had finished it. Pozzi's bronze reliefs have more dignity, at any rate, and so has the head of a steer which supports one end of the Table. The Assumpta Galerie, immediately behind the Hochaltar, is ornamented by four allegorical statues, the work of J. B. Babel, whose gift for nonchalant grandeur we have already remarked in the Klosterplatz. They are of varying merit, but it is difficult not to recognize in the figure of Abundance, and in her forceful way with the cornucopia, the presiding spirit of those who built this church. Babel's masterpieces, however, lie in the gallery which runs above the choir. Here stand, rather larger than life, the Apostles. Pen in hand, or surprised in a moment of anguished reverie, these bearded giants give one the authentic sense that they alone could transmit the Word. They dignify, indeed almost mortify, their surroundings; for at this point the architecture of Einsiedeln is in danger—not serious danger, but danger none the less—of going off. Babel's angels should also be remarked, for just occasionally he mingles with the tubby seraphs of Bavarian convention a tormented adolescent more appropriate to the mythology of our own age (67).

I have by no means completed the catalogue of this extraordinary abbey. If I neglect the choir-stalls in the Oberechor, carved between 1675 and 1680 by Michael Hartmann of Lucerne, it is because English visitors will have good standards of their own by which to recognize their quality; and if I neglect the wall-paintings in the same place, which are by the brothers Torricelli from Lugano, it is not because I do not appreciate the easy sufficiency of the work, or the almost flippant rapidity with which it was completed. I could write at length of the work of Diego Carlone, a sculptor from Acaria, near Como, who worked at Einsiedeln from 1730 to 1738, executing eight side-altars and two large allegorical funeral tablets. Allegories came easily to Carlone. Prudence, Justice and Hope are resolved, in his sculptures and reliefs, into handsome women in the prime of life (Stendhalian *âmes fortes*, as often as not); and they are rendered with a melodious sensuality far removed from the tight and guilty handling which such subjects assume in more northerly climes. One cannot suspect, before Carlone's cherubs, as one can before the work of other sculptors, that the artist is ignorant of the possibilities of undress. Nor is he overawed by a great subject; one might protest, indeed, that in his hands the Mount of Olives becomes a country excursion and the Passion a party of pleasure; but at best there is everywhere the loose-running, light-reined sense of form, and leaning upon it the vividest, most outspoken affirmation of the beauty and variety of the human body. Carlone is one of the surprises of Einsiedeln; but his share in the building is a very minor one, and rather than leave the great church upon so uncharacteristic a note, I shall urge the reader before he leaves to mount (for this, one must apply in advance) to one of the galleries; for from there alone can he savour to the full the aerial imagination which makes Einsiedeln such a memorable experience.

The church, moreover, is only a small part of the abbey. One must walk all round it (and also, if possible, in the interior gardens), noting where fragments of H. J. Kuen's designs of the 1670s remain

68   Einsiedeln : the Choir Screen (1675-85 ;
designer, Vinzenz Nussbaumer) and the Choir

69   Vineyards in the Veltlin

70   Haymaking in the Ticino

to grace the west door of the former Belchtkirche, and how on the north façade was incorporated one side of the hexagon which Caspar Moosbrugger built, in his earliest years at the abbey, as an appendix to the Magdalenenkapelle. One must note how at times the buildings take on the seignorial air of a great country house. The west front, for example, has the untroubled assurance of a house so grand that it need not bother to assert itself; fittingly it enshrines the arms of Abbot Maurus von Roll, by whose energy and thrift the present buildings were launched. At once palace and garrison, the abbey proves how flexible a great style of building can be. Within, the corridors are as bare as any ascete could wish; but watch the proportions of the overdoors and the alternation of oval and octagon in the stuccoed ceiling. Only in the guest-room do hospitable habits allow of some imaginary landscapes in stucco, done by J. A. Feuchtmayr in 1738; this fertile Bavarian also worked in the library, a room designed—and with a touching, rather amateurish grace—by two members of the abbey, both natives of Porrentruy, in 1738. When we have explored in the Fürstensaal, we can profitably turn to the other history of the abbey: the tradition of discreet excellence in learning, music and pageantry; the festivals of the Church, whose rich cycle suffuses the life of a whole countryside; the inward obedience and the outward joy—aspects of the religious experience which find perfected expression at Einsiedeln. Not all visitors may relish this kind of expression; but let them in that case make an effort of understanding. No style, after all, is quite what it seems; and those who find in baroque nothing but profane amenity should ponder the lesson of Henry Adams who was, with Henry James, the most passionate of all transatlantic students of Europe. Adams knew that one must allow for some delay in admiration. The Normans, for instance: "As they slowly reveal themselves, they disclose most unexpected qualities; one seems to sound subterranean caverns of feeling hidden behind their iron nasals." There are no iron nasals at Einsiedeln; but there are caverns of feeling to be sounded, none the less.

VI

The Ticino

The Ticinese Valleys—Lake Lugano—Ascona—Bellinzona

THE Ticino canton covers a great deal of ground—from the granite ocean of the Gotthard plateau to the maize-flats of the Lombard plain. Skilful publicity has made it seem a paradise on earth, and it is true that on Lake Lugano and on the northern half of Lake Maggiore one can counterfeit the pleasures of an ideal Riviera. Nothing in Switzerland is more surprising than the hotel at Ascona, with Picasso in the lift and Juan Gris in the second-best bedroom; nothing more bemusing than the orange-scented gardens of Morcote; nothing more Italian, outside of Italy, than the octagonal cupola of the Santa Croce Church at Riva San Vitale. All these induce an oriental languor in the tourist, and constitute, indeed, almost an ordeal of pleasure. But they are only a very small part of the Ticino, which would more rationally be remembered as a country of inhospitable valleys in which the sun rebounds from rock to rock and the visitor is regarded, as often as not, with plain-spoken dislike. Few and chastened are they who have reached the end of the Val di Vergeletto or the Val Antabbia, for these are regions remote from the well-organized Eldorado of the lakes; and as the sun vanishes at three o'clock beneath some glowering peak, many a stumbling pedestrian must envisage himself reduced to the pabulum ascribed by Wordsworth to the earliest Christians in the Vaud:

> *herbs self-sown,*
> *And fruitage gathered from the chestnut wood.*

The inhabitants of these valleys are, in the main, disagreeable people with plenty to be disagreeable about. Their mode of life is stationary, and has been so for several hundred years. Many of their villages can only be reached, even now, with extreme difficulty; in certain areas a rope-and-wire bridge over a sixty-foot drop is luxury. Yet the tourist, be he sufficiently hardy, can plunge with great profit into the noonday furnace of the Val Bavona or the Val Verzasca; for it is there, rather than in the groomed and scented resorts of the lakeside, that the broad arcades and open bell-towers of the Ticino can be seen as they deserve. One of the Ticinese valleys is well known to

nearly every Swiss visitor, for the Val Leventina is part of the
Gotthard road; but for every thousand travellers who will have been
able to see, at Giornico, the exemplary Romanesque Church of
S. Niccolò, hardly one will have turned aside to the adjacent Val
Blenio in order to examine its little contemporary, the Church of
S. Remigio at Corzoneso. These other valleys lead nowhere. The
road pushes obstinately forward through the chestnut forests, works
its way round the great thumbs of rock which threaten to push it off
the map, encounters every ten miles another crumbling stone village,
and finally peters out at a point where suddenly the walls of rock
decide to converge from right and left. There are several reasons for
exploring them, none the less. One is that the experience is in salutary
contrast to the extreme and professional amiability of Lugano and
its satellites. Another, that along these desolate tracks one meets
with startling evidence of the Ticinese gift for building and decoration. Histories of the area often quote the names of local architects
who throve in foreign parts, and were given the chance to refine and
concentrate their powers—Domenico Fontana, whose hand may be
seen in the Vatican; Carlo Maderna, who built the façade of St.
Peter's; Baldassare Longhena, the architect of Sta. Maria della
Salute in Venice; Pietro Solari, who worked on the Kremlin, and
Domenico Trezzini who was employed on the great ensembles at
St. Petersburg. These are proud names, but they did not do more
honour to the Ticino than the countless minor artists, many of them
now unknown, who ornamented this wild countryside, not only with
churches but with the wayside chapels which are the special contribution of the Ticino to Swiss architecture. It is the combination of
these arresting and unheeded objects with a landscape of singular
wildness and grandeur that persuades some visitors to break away
from where

fair Locarno smiles
Embowered in walnut slopes and citron isles.

Few of these wayside chapels are included in Dr. Jenny's survey,
and indeed it is difficult to class them, for there are no accepted
canons by which they might be judged. They derive in part from
painting, in part from architecture. Essentially they are frescoes,
with some form of tent or canopy to protect them from the weather.
A few of them are found in or near villages, or even at the churchyard
gate; but open country is their natural home. Sometimes a complete
tabernacle, the size of a small signalman's box, has been erected in
their honour, and a few art-conscious neighbourhoods have even

put iron bars between us and them. But these are unworthy and recent precautions; the true *cappelle* go unprotected. Two, often three centuries have so weathered them that they seem an organic part of their surroundings; the artist's ornamental border, his scrolls and flourishes, have merged into the equally ornamental patina of worn stone and flaked plaster; and the yearly alternation of sunshine and snow has cracked the careful pediment and allowed the weeds to flower through the floor. Sometimes the ground has eroded away, leaving the Virgin and her attendants high above the road; sometimes society has closed in upon the chapel and strung its telephone wires above the roof; sometimes the painted fruit upon the architrave are partnered by the real cherries which overhang them from the loaded bough. Fresco is not the only medium employed in these chapels, though it is the most common. There may be groups in painted wood as at Brissago, stucco figures in high relief as at Rovio, statuary in plaster as at Melide, or painted panels of wood. The custom persisted even far into the nineteenth century, when G. A. Vanoni painted the chapels at Antrobbia, in the Val Maggia and at Aurigeno. But his was not a good period, and it is the chapels of the seventeenth and eighteenth centuries which will give most pleasure; for in these it is possible to match the golden age of decoration against the Cisalpine landscape in which we first glimpsed the possibilities of colour. Of course these nameless painters were not men of very great gifts; nor is the Ticinese landscape comparable in delicacy to that of Tuscany; but it is none the less an extraordinary sensation to contemplate the success with which these rude chapels have taken painting into Nature. They have been little studied until recently; but with the aid of M. Piero Banconi's excellent book the tourist can devise for himself an itinerary which will yield, I dare forecast, many an unsuspected pleasure.

Time and the elements have drained off much of what must once have been the violent colour of these frescoes. Within doors, this is of course not the case; and there are few churches in the Ticino which will not disclose, in the hue and extent of their ornamentation, an extreme aggressiveness of taste. It is not a question of the

Inexplicable splendour of Ionian white and gold

but of a childlike, barbaric confusion in which gold and scarlet fight for their lives in a general mêlée of colour. These interiors have always been considered beyond the pale of serious criticism; but fashion has been edging in their direction, and it would not surprise me if my successors in the year 2000 were to give them deferential

71, 72   Chapels in the Ticino

73 Bellinzona : the late fifteenth-century fortifications

attention. Churches apart, the villages of the Ticino are not of great interest. Their charm derives from the cunning with which Nature has been called in to soften the outlines of bare, unornamented stone. Nowhere is there a greater profusion of arbours, nowhere are balconies more densely entwined with flowers and vines; for this is poor country. Nobody has ever had much money to spend in the Ticino; and if they had, it would have been difficult to make Sonvico and Roveredo into places of amenity. Visitors may mount, out of curiosity, to these lofty hamlets; and they may admire the view, and the silent passion with which, in an alleyway bordered with flowering shrubs, the inhabitants give themselves over to their local variant of bowls. But before nightfall they will scramble down again to Lugano, or Morcote, or Campione, or Melide; and who should blame them?

Lugano is like Blackpool—it gives in full measure what people expect of it, and those who dislike it are not compelled to go. It reached its maximum at the turn of the century and is not likely to develop beyond its present state. Originally the preferred resort of the retired German shopkeeper, it still offers the spectacle of a large pleasure-resort, built on to a small Swiss-Italian town. It is the kind of town for which excuses are made; and the irritable, dissatisfied few are sent to look at the Old Town—the arcades, the Luini frescoes, the "quaint" market and so forth. This procedure raises the most damning objection of all—namely, that there is nothing in Lugano, or anywhere along the lakes, which cannot be had in greater strength and better quality in Italy itself. And the Ticino is not Italy. This is more than a geographical quibble—a whole principle of life is in question. French Switzerland is something in itself, and German Switzerland something more; but Italian Switzerland. . . . One must say in fairness that few people would second this view; nearly everybody who goes to Lugano has a delightful time and lives only for the moment when they can go again. Also in fairness I must assert that, banal as it may be, Lugano when compared with Como is like Eden before the Fall. But then everybody is blind to something, and I can honestly protest innocence of any initial prejudice against these celebrated playgrounds. Quite the contrary, indeed: no one was more ready to enjoy a landscape over which Nature had bent like an antique figure of Abundance, pouring all her best endowments upon three narrow strips of favoured ground; no one looked forward more eagerly to the society of vivacious *indigènes*, each speaking the language of d'Annunzio and wreathed in a Mediterranean smile; and no one was relying so credulously upon the absolute tranquillity of the lakes, the sense of a world from which fatigue and guilt were replaced by a pagan euphoria. And many people do find all these things in the Ticino, just as one commentator has found that the Ticino itself, in the plain below Bellinzona, goes towards Lake Maggiore like "a virgin towards her nuptial bed". Nor should one suggest that the two statements are on the same level of extravagance. But it remains possible to dislike Lugano, Stresa, Como and the rest, and to resent the fact that more interesting places in other parts of Switzerland have always been played down in deference to an area in which practically everything is either barbaric or second-rate. This said, I must own that the popularity of Ascona (75, 76) is not surprising. This little fishing village faces due south, at the top of Lake Maggiore, and it contains at any rate one façade of great interest— that of the Casa Borrani, built in 1620, and ornamented with plaster groups above its first-floor windows; but even that, as Dr. Jenny implies, has been done better elsewhere.

As Bellinzona (73, 74) is the capital of the Ticino and most people will pass through it on their way back from the canton, it is no more than polite to examine the town. An extreme, perhaps deceptive lassitude envelops the residential quarters of Bellinzona, and the Piazza Independénza is like nothing so much as a suburb of Athens; but in the centre of the town there are signs, few but distinct, that Swiss elements are regaining ground. A polished inn-sign, the *Neue Zürcher Zeitung* in a café, a good-hearted attempt to clean the streets—all foreshadow the changed mode of life which obtains across the Bernardino Pass. Churches follow suit: the Collegiate Church of SS. Pietro e Stefano has a façade remodelled in the 1650s in which something is actually left to the observer's imagination. The grave spaces and unforced dignity of this building are most imposing after an area in which churches force one's admiration by half-drowning themselves in vulgarity and coming out, practically unscathed, on the far side. But of course the chief curiosity of Bellinzona is the three great castles which dominate the town. The gap-toothed monsters are in good repair and recall the time, early in the fifteenth century, when the Confederates fought the Duke of Milan for possession of the upper valley of the Ticino. The struggle went on for fifty years, with temporary advantage to one side or the other. The first blow was struck in 1403, when the Confederates seized the Val Leventina. This was a great moment in Swiss history—partly because, for the first time, an Italian-speaking people was incorporated into the hitherto German-speaking groups, and partly also because it inaugurated a new epoch of expansion. Within twenty years they had taken over all the strategic points in what is now the Ticino, and were in control of every pass which led down to the Lombard plain. In 1422 the Milanese hit back, and after defeating

74 Bellinzona : façade of the Collegiate Church, largely rebuilt in 1654

75, 76 In the town (*left*),
and (*below*) on the waterfront

the Confederates at Arbedo, they recaptured all the valleys south of the Alps. Only the people of Uri still wanted to go on with the fight; the rest of the Swiss were content with diplomacy, but for double security the Duke of Milan decided to combine the three castles of Bellinzona with a chain of minor fortifications, and so to seal off the valley of the Ticino from any invader. Four of the best military engineers in Italy were employed on the job, and it is recorded that in 1460 Aristotile Fieraranti from Bologna, the greatest military architect of the day, came specially to examine the result. Impressive as it still is, it did not prevent the Swiss from retaking Bellinzona in 1503, and in September 1513 Locarno, Lugano and Mendrisio also became part of the Confederation. The fortifications of Bellinzona have been carefully preserved and still present an arresting spectacle —though not one in keeping with the general idea of the Ticino. Myself impervious to the spell of the area, I must wish my readers better fortune. May they inhabit ideal villas beneath a blistering sun; may their risottos be free from pebbles and grit; may their sheets be quite clean, and the pages of their French novels already cut; and when they go walking, may they happen upon a church on whose outer walls time has reduced some hideous fresco to a many-coloured and evocative stain. Then are they sure to enjoy the Ticino.

VII

The Grisons

The Engadine—Chur—The Rhine Valley—Disentis

THE Grisons are inmost, nethermost Switzerland. They form the largest of the cantons, and the one which is perhaps most dear to English travellers. In winter and summer alike, the Engadine is surely the most coveted of all valleys, and Davos Klosters, St. Moritz and Arosa the favourite resorts of all but a minority of our fellow-countrymen. Myself largely ignorant of them, I incline therefore to leave the Grisons in better hands, for they are best described by those who excel in the strenuosities of the Parsenn and the Cresta. Of course one does not need skis to appreciate the high-lying valley of the Inn, the grilling winter sunshine, and the peaks of the Bernina, unimaginably bright and clear at a distance of twenty miles. But these things have been done very well before; and the eulogies of Symonds and Stevenson—not to mention the breathless reporting of H. E. G. Tyndale and Peter Lunn—could certainly not be bettered by me, who have never seen the Engadine in summer and could only peer irritably at Pontresina through a blinding snowstorm. Regret has its visions, though, as much as memory; and the unvisited National Park in the Lower Engadine, with its roebuck and capricorn, the Italianate palaces of the de Salis family at Bondo and Soglio, and the well-loved lakes at Silvaplana and Sils-Maria—these are more familiar to my imagination than many places long known with the outward eye. Laziness and love of tobogganing caused some of these defections; bad weather and mechanical breakdowns may justify others. But the Grisons cover a lot of ground —and ground, moreover, so intensely serrated that it would take years to explore every valley; and so special, so timeless is the life of these distant hamlets that it is the merest self-deception to suppose that a visitor can penetrate it. At most he is borne politely on its outer surface. He may be made welcome in the evening, when the red Veltliner passes round, the long black cheroots glow gradually into ash, and the ancient symbolism of the Tarot pack reassumes its spell over the lamp-lit table. There may be signs of material change; the wireless may pour out its futilities in an adjoining room, and a prehistoric telephone may stand on some lofty pedestal; but life in the Grisons has a stalagmitic quality which puts it outside our own experience. Only those who have lived there, and perforce adapted the pace of their being to that of their surroundings, can begin to comprehend it. Yet it can be done—and was done, for example, by Llewellyn Powys, whose *Swiss Essays* detail, with the passionate exactness of one who has not long to live, the structure of life in the Grisons. Powys first came to this country as a young man; he returned, in his last years, to the upland meadows where, as he all too aptly quoted:

> *All the flowers of the spring*
> *Meet to perfume our burying.*

The obvious excitements of winter-sporting are replaced in this book by the deep-breathing economy of a way of life which has outlasted many great changes in the world and is likely to remain, a remonstrance Biblical in its plainness, as long as the world itself.

In the face of the timeless life of the Grisons, with its rich symbolism and cunning, slightly zanyish conventions, one cannot feel great pride at the contributions of its English admirers. Mrs. Gaskell must be given a good mark for having written *Wives and Daughters* at Pontresina; but writers must wince to recall that their great colleague Sir Arthur Conan Doyle was responsible for laying out the golf-course at Davos. As if there was not enough golf in the world already! (Nietzsche, at Sils-Maria, was at least putting forth all his powers.) Do the golfers, one wonders, notice any difference between Davos and Moor Park? The unwinking gaze of the young-eyed consumptive is a better guide.

Powys notes down many curious and attaching facts about the people of the Grisons: their passion for night-long dancing on wedding-days; the tiny aperture, or soul-window, carved above the ordinary windows in order that, after death, the soul may slip through unhindered on its way to heaven; and crueller customs, such as that of strewing autumn crocuses outside the house of a girl suspected of unchastity. But society is only a small part of Grison life. Solitary pleasures occupy much of the book—the observation of chamois, marmot and mountain fox; the awful spectacle of a blizzard in the forest, when "the very mice are mum at the ends of their tiny tunnels, their rodent flesh and blood experiencing a conjured oblivion under well-fitting thumb-large jerkins of thickly grown winter fur"; the terrible span—more than eight feet across—of the wings of the Steinadler, as it treads the air in search of a new trophy for its ancestral nest, coated through the years with "the putrid maggoty remains of goats, sheep, roe-deer, chamois, badgers, foxes, marmots, hares and snow-chicken"; the routine, so strange to English eyes, of hay-making in the high valleys; and the surprising pasturage on the very mountain-tops—"in midsummer, when the flowers are in blossom, to walk across these Alps is like being abroad on the wide paradise-back of Olympus".

Where Nature has shown herself in such idiosyncratic form, Man has not lagged behind. The Grisons contain architecture of every sort, from the German step-roofed country house (Schloss Bothmar at Malans) to the houses of Andeer and Filisur, riotous with graffiti, and the little Church of Sta. Maria outside Poschiavo (80) which was laid out in 1708 in the purest Mediterranean style, with cypresses to give it shade and a campanile from which the bell rings out freely down the valley of the Bernina and into Italy. Often—Zuoz is the great example (77)—there is a local architecture, indestructibly solid, embellished with the exquisite handwriting of a distant century, often stamped with the great name of the neighbourhood, and boasting at times a roof-line such as a master-calligrapher might have drawn. In such towns one can disregard the signatures of our own century. The Lower Engadine, less visited than the higher reaches of the valley, yet contains exquisite examples of vernacular architecture. Schuls itself can show several in the Dorfplatz; and three miles away, in the Val Sinestra, is the village of Sent, remarkable even in Switzerland for the number of times it has been laid waste by fire. A sevenfold scourge has been laid upon Sent. The blows, spaced out between 1499 and 1921, leave few old houses intact; but conspicuous among so much newness are some fine specimens of rusticated elegance. These date from the period immediately following the fire of 1823, and they are called the Haus Gianom, Men Poo and the Gasthaus Helvetia. But the Grisons have so heterogeneous a character that every one of their extremities is interesting. Due south from Schuls, for instance, there is a pocket of Switzerland enisled in Italy; and in this is the Frauenkloster St. Johann Baptista, a foundation dating from the last quarter of the eighth century. This was one of the earliest Benedictine foundations in Switzerland (only Reichenau, St. Gall and Disentis date from the same century) and it was the first of the Benedictine convents. It is also the oldest monastic building in the country.

Directly north of Münster, again, there is a small German-speaking pocket, with the lofty hamlet of Samnaun for its capital. I cannot claim that it has any arresting monuments, but on the southern leg of the perimeter of the Grisons there are two Italian-speaking pockets. I have already vaunted the charms of Poschiavo; let me couple with them the beauties of Vicosoprano, which lies in the Val

77 Zuoz : the main street

78 A village church near Davos

79   Maienfeld : the thirteenth-century tower of the Schloss von Brandis

80   Poschiavo : the Church of Sta. Maria (1708-12)

Bregaglia, a luxuriant valley surrounded by mountain walls of 10,000 to 11,000 feet in height. Vicosoprano is that agreeable thing—a tiny capital, now of no significance, but still bearing the mark of its former dignities. How else, after all, could we interpret the town hall, upon which, in the late sixteenth century, sgraffiti figures of Virtue and Temperance were lovingly inlaid; and for those who disregarded the injunctions of these monitors, an ingenious lock-up was constructed in the interior of the building; a whipping-post and two gallows-trees complete the cautionary equipment of the village. Where dignities are concerned, however, Maienfeld, the northernmost town in the Grisons, can boast an excellent supply (79).

I have picked out these border-towns in order to show how the Grisons reproduced nearly all Switzerland in miniature. Certainly the mountains are there, and the long, black-shaded valleys, and the juxtaposition of three languages within an hour's ride by train; the inexpugnable, basic Switzerland is there, with its lifelong combat against nature and geography; and the political history is there, with its serpentine intrigues, and its long wars, as unaccountable to a summer tourist as are the battles in Shakespeare to a Bulgarian visitor to Stratford. What is lacking is the massive intellectual power which, elsewhere in Switzerland, has raised provincial towns to the stature of Heidelberg or Bonn. Not that I wish to slight the University of Chur—so profuse is its curriculum, so ardent its nurslings; but there is beyond question a dullness in long residence at high altitudes, and the wisdom of an unlettered peasantry is not, in this academic sense, a substitute for the practised intelligence of Fribourg and St. Gall. Moreover, the difficulty of life in the Grisons persuades many of the élite of the canton to seek fortune elsewhere; and those foreign visitors who are not compelled for medical reasons to remain above 5,000 feet may well begin to fret when the climate provokes them to a frenzy of intellectual curiosity which the outward scene—dare I forecast?—will fail to satisfy. Meanwhile, there are remarkable things to be seen—the Rhine valley, freckled with castles from Thusis to Sargans, the gratifying torments of the Via Mala, and the dead landscape at the top of the Oberalp. There are good things to eat—the dark-red slices of Bündnerfleisch, thin as India paper and equal to the finest English bacon; and the Birnbrot, a cake which weathers like oak and is made with thin slices of dried pear, hazel-nuts, almonds, raisins, cloves, cinnamon and nutmeg. It is good to munch this bizarre but succulent vittle as the train passes through the limestone defile of the Rhine above Chur, or one lies in blissful hebetude in fine-edged meadow-grass below Flims. For the Grisons include almost every variety of sensuous life—from the compulsive languor of the lower Bernina valley to the unrewarded rigours of the highest uplands. To the visitor who can lay aside formal manners, the countryside offers many possibilities of pagan enjoyment—of the *Nourritures Terrestres*, in short, which André Gide has evoked with such disturbing power. And Gide himself, though no general enthusiast for Swiss pastimes, has appreciated the flower-strewn life of the Grison meadows. In August 1894 he wrote from Chur to Paul Valéry: *"Je suis heureux ce soir, car cet après-midi je me baignai tout nu dans un vert torrent de montagne ; pour me sécher, après, je me roulai dans l'herbe chaude."* Fifty years later this became part of the gamut of pleasure with which Gide endowed his Theseus; and Theseus, looking back on his youth, could say: *"Alors que je me sentais si bien, assis à cru sur l'herbe fraîche. . . ."*

Hawthorne and Norman Douglas have memorably analysed the effect of Mediterranean manners upon those who have been formed in less ardent moulds. If nobody has done the same for Switzerland, it is probably because the underground messages of the senses have usually been snubbed or disregarded in these strenuous cantons. Switzerland is a country, as Mr. Cyril Connolly has very aptly remarked, in which "all Nature cries 'Forgive yourself!' and Man, defiant, answers 'Never!' " Exercise is the classical, Arnoldian sedative for the demands of the senses, and only occasionally does one glimpse that all may not be well. Henry James, always an incomparable truffle-hound in such contexts, noted, on March 26th, 1884, the motive particle of gossip which, originally relating to J. A. Symonds and his life at Davos, was later transfused into *The Author of Beltraffio*. "Edmund Gosse," wrote James in his notebook, "was speaking of J. A. S., the writer . . . of his extreme and somewhat hysterical æstheticism, etc.: the sad conditions of his life, exiled to Davos by the state of his lungs, the illness of his daughter, etc. 'I have never read any of John's works. I think them most *undesirable*.' " Such glimpses redouble the curiosity of Symonds' declaration that "neither Rome nor the Riviera wins our hearts like Switzerland. We do not lie awake in London thinking of them; we do not long so intensely, as the year comes round, to revisit them. Our affection is less a passion than that which we cherish for Switzerland. Why, then, is this?"

Why, indeed? The question must interest even those who, like myself, would incline to reverse Symonds' affirmation. Of course, the first and grandest of reasons is that the Englishman is made to feel at home in Switzerland. Elsewhere the empire of the Milord has fallen in ruins; the prestige of Bristol and Edward VII no longer obtains; but in Switzerland an Englishman may still feel himself the

81   Spring crocuses in the Engadine

82 Disentis: the Abbey
(*c.* 1685; *architect, Caspar Moosbrugger*) (*left*)

83 Chur: a general view
(*below*)

first citizen of the world. There is some justice in this kindly pretence, for the Swiss tourist industry has always been based in large
part upon English custom. No sooner does an English visitor heave
into view in a train, a restaurant, or the lounge, heavy with plush, of
an Alpine hotel, than his Swiss neighbours will begin to lard their
conversation with English phrases; this amiable though rather
simian habit is the index, it seems to me, of their benevolent interest
in our affairs. The charm of Switzerland, over and above its scenic,
monumental and gastronomic advantages (each of which can be
bettered by one of her neighbours) derives from the fact that all
human beings long for respect and affection; and they have a better
chance of finding them, on sight, in Switzerland than anywhere else
in Europe. Moreover, the problem of language hardly exists between
these boundaries, where even the analphabetic finds a welcome.

The Grisons are good testing-ground for these assertions. It is a
good plan to attack them from the south. Henry James, whom I
quote so freely because few have expressed themselves so well,
always remembered a journey over the Splügen—"I shall never
forget the sensation of rising as night came (I walked incessantly,
after we began to ascend) into that cool pure Alpine air, out of the
stifling *calidarium* of Italy." The San Bernardino Pass should also be
experienced—beginning with the first level stretch, out of Bellinzona,
through fields strewn with golden pumpkins; in these same fields, in
1422, three thousand Swiss fought gallantly against a Milanese army
six times as large as their own; large mounds still mark their graves.
Entering next the narrow cleft of the Val Calanca, we soon sight the
castle of Mesocco. This imposing ruin, so dear to Samuel Butler,
was built by the family of Sax-Misox, from whom Mesocco takes its
name. They sold it in 1483 to a Milanese general, and forty years
later the enraged population of the Grisons destroyed it. It has at
present the authentic Office-of-Works appearance of well-kept
dereliction, and it serves mainly to mark off the Italianate end of the
Moesa valley from the beginning of the Pass proper. Mesocco,
through which the goats pass like castanets, is best examined for the
Church of S. Maria del Castello. Easily recognizable by its Romanesque bell-tower, this church boasts at once a raftered ceiling with
baroque decoration and a series of late-fifteenth-century frescoes,
much admired by Samuel Butler and well described in his fervent,
agreeably cranky *Alps and Sanctuaries*.

As the road mounts and the trees drop away, and on the topmost
pink rocks the chamois deigns to slip past our questing field-glasses,
the character of the villages changes also. The villages of Italian
Switzerland are not squalid with the irredeemable, life-accepting

squalor of real Italian villages, but they are squalid none the less. Already at San Bernardino the resources of life are enlarged. Striped umbrellas lurk among the pines, and the shallow-domed church (unaccountably omitted, with the whole town, from Dr. Jenny's survey) inaugurates a countryside in which something may conceivably be going forward; as the villas of Bellinzona drop away, with their roofs trimmed with white-painted wedding-cake ironwork, the sticky heat drops away also, and with it the ever-trickling gutters, the Hogarthian alley-ways, and the idiot children lolling in the shade. When the great climb is over, and we are free to coast down towards the valley of the Rhine, a new world is open to us. Hinterrhein is not in itself an exciting village, but it is the first village on the upper Rhine; as such, it has adapted its colouring to the elephant-grey affected at this stage by the Rhine itself, and only by a brilliantly polished inn-sign, and the as brilliant blue-and-gold of the face on the church clock, do we recognize the beginning of the carnival of shining cleanliness which is the mark of the Swiss Rhineland. More interesting villages will appear on the road towards Chur—Zillis, for example, in which the Kirche St. Martin should be sought out. This church was founded in 940, and although the structure has been very considerably modified, the flat ceiling of the nave is ornamented with no fewer than 140 painted panels, dating from the first half of the twelfth century, and restored in 1939–40 to a degree of finish elsewhere known only in Sir Arthur Evans's reconstruction of Cnossos. Visitors should not fail to decipher the panels in which are portrayed, with the decorative calligraphy of the practised illuminator, scenes from the Revelation and the New Testament; Dr. Jenny encourages us to find in these "amphibious Fable-creatures upon a stormy sea". The trumpeting angels of the Apocalypse, and the two panels depicting scenes from the life of St. Martin, will also give pleasure, and the church as a whole forms an arresting interlude in a day spent in the warm basin of the valley.

Of the larger Grison monuments, the Benedictine Abbey of Disentis and the Cathedral at Chur are the most important. They are separated by the length of the Vorder Rhein valley, off which run other, smaller valleys to north and south—the Panixer Tal, known to Suvorow, the Somvixer Tal, wild with cherries in summer, the Val Puntaiglas, closed by glaciers, and the egregious Via Mala, thick with mouldering castles. Disentis itself (82) is a victim of the apathy so common in the Grisons when circumstances call for a general change of habits. It is beautifully, indeed radiantly situated on the hillside, facing the Medel glacier and the peaks (9,000 feet and upwards) of the Piz Valdraus and the Piz Vial. The view along the valley, with its endless recessions of green and blue, is sometimes of magical beauty, and there are valuable and enlivening springs of iron-bearing, radio-active waters, which would have made the fortune of a more enter-prising town. The abbey is voted "plain and dull" by those who themselves deserve these epithets; there is such a thing as a noble plainness, and this is a case in point. Moreover, the interior of the church, which was built between 1696 and 1762 to a plan in which Caspar Moosbrugger had probably collaborated, is perfectly in keeping; for the voluptuous inventions of Einsiedeln and St. Gall are here subdued, and there results a building monumental in its squareness, flawed by recent and copious restoration (the paintings are the most hideous of any to be found in a Swiss church of this stature) and often heavy in its detail; but for all that an honest, robust achievement, and a princely addition to this rich countryside.

Chur (83) is a town in which nobody stays longer than he need. It is not positively unpleasant; it just does have the character of a town which people leave as quickly as they can. No doubt this is why its hotels and restaurants are mostly very poor. There is something not to be missed, none the less, in the quays along the dilatory Plessur, and on the Mittenberg—the high mound which is sur-mounted by the Cathedral, the Bishop's Palace and the Martins-kirche. Chur was once a rich town. Like Brigue and Lucerne, it fattened on the great caravans which loitered within its boundaries before going south to Italy by the Splügen or the Julier Pass. More: it was a town of consequence even in Roman times, with a castle on the Mittenberg. To-day it is still an important junction, with a station buffet of great excellence, and a number of fine sixteenth-century houses in the narrow alleys in the middle of the town. The cathedral is a kind of ecclesiastical anthology, in which there is something for every taste. Thirteen centuries have contributed to the building as it now stands. It is built upon uneven ground, and in plan is notably unsymmetrical. Excavation has revealed the founda-tions of two separate apses beneath the choir—one dating from the second half of the eighth century, the other from an even earlier epoch. The existing cathedral was built between 1150 and 1265. The Chapel of St. Lawrence was built on to the south aisle in the late fifteenth century, and at this time was added also the sumptuous carved screen above the altar. This is by Jakob Russ of Ravensburg, and Dr. Jenny calls it "the finest and most elaborate carved altar in Switzerland". Careful polychromatic decorations in nave and aisles, fragments of Carolingian reliefs, Romanesque capitals, funerary sculpture of the seventeenth and eighteenth centuries, modern stained glass, early fifteenth-century choir-stalls and an uncommonly rich and varied treasure by no means complete the resources of this extraordinary edifice; the opportunity of a halt between trains should never be missed by those who enjoy a certain luminous inconsistency in architecture.

Several of the old streets of Chur, and the enclosed squares (hardly more than wells between the overhanging roofs of the sixteenth century) retain something of the pressure of the heroic age in the history of the town. I have not space to describe the long struggle by which, in the fifteenth century, Chur threw off its bondage to the Bishops of Chur and broke free, also, from its secular overlords. The ruined castles along the Rhine are the best memorial to this strenuous period. Nor shall I trace the career of Jürg Jenatsch, who was born at Samaden in 1596, and grew up to become the saviour of the Grisons at the time, some forty years later, when they became the battle-field upon which the power of Spain and Austria was pitted against that of Venice and France. Professor G. R. de Beer has given, in his *Escape to Switzerland,* an admirable and detailed account of this struggle, which was exacerbated by the internal complication that the Catholic Swiss, headed by the Plantas, were partisans of one side, and the Protestants of the other. In nearly every Englishman there is hiding somewhere an Old Liberal, and this kindly figure is bound to be hurt when we discover, as we generally do, that a great national hero has been violent, even dishonest, in his conduct of affairs. Jenatsch was an odious man, but an invaluable one; and though one dislikes to think of so useful a servant of Swiss liberty being cut to pieces in a tavern brawl (in Chur, too), it would have been surprising if he had been allowed to die in his bed. From 1525, the Grisons had been a considerable, though minor, power in Europe. Mr. Arnold Lunn has described, with the ardour of lifelong affection, how this came about. "The conquest of the Valtelline, coveted by both France and Austria, gave to the rulers of the Grisons a position of European importance. Davos sent its ambassadors to the courts of Paris and Vienna and its proconsuls to rule over the subject Italian provinces. The great families of Davos, the Buols and the Gulers, for instance, whose descendants are well known to British visitors, were ennobled by kings, and their portraits in armour or in ambassadorial dress still survive. They were men of great culture, writing an easy and elegant Latin; but though aristocrats when abroad, they were careful when at home to maintain a life of Spartan and Republican simplicity." It is this residue of wealth and cultivation which prevents the towns and villages of the Grisons from appearing insignificant in relation to the scenic extravagances of Nature.

84   The medieval Castle of Werdenberg, seat of the Counts of Werdenberg

85　Stein-am-Rhein : the Marktplatz

VIII

Basle, St. Gall and the Bodensee

Basle—The Rhine—Schaffhausen—Arenenberg—The Bodensee—
St. Gall

BASLE has never been a welcoming city. The basilisk, indeed, figures as appropriately in the arms of Basle as does the sun in the arms of Sierre, or the friendly bear in those of Berne. Those who are at first dispirited by this lack of amenity may be consoled by the thought that some of Basle's most honoured connections have begun in the same way. Consider Nietzsche, boxed up in a servant's bedroom for the first two months of his professorship. Consider the French traveller who remarked, some thirty years earlier, that "at Basle every shutter is closed at the sound of a travelling coach and every woman hides herself. Everything is dead and deserted. A city to let, one might say." A wise traveller will not put up in the centre of the main town, nor even in the palatial Drei Könige. From the waterfront of Klein Basel—or, better, from a balcony above the street, he will gaze across two hundred yards of water to where, on the steep bluffs which overhang the other bank of the Rhine, the city shows its best side. Moreover, history has flouted geography by making this great stretch of water the real centre of Basle. In Celtic times a settlement of fishermen, hunters and boatmen was established at the point where the Birsig (now as well hidden as the Fleet) flows into the Rhine. Here Erasmus embarked for Cologne, in the autumn of 1518, and was harassed by flies as he dined at Breisach. Here the victorious Bohemians arrived by water from Schaffhausen on January 4th, 1433, to find that gambling, dancing and association with prostitutes had been rigorously proscribed in expectation of their arrival. Here, in October of the same year, the Emperor Sigismund arrived by boat on the last stage of his journey from Rome. This period of the Council of Basle was one of the most brilliant in the history of the city, but unfortunately it is rarely taught in English schools. (Even Randall Creighton, the author of the canonical *History of the Papacy*, disliked Switzerland and seems never to have been to Basle.) From 1424 until 1448 Basle was, with Rome, one of the two great cities of Europe. Within the previous hundred years it had survived a plague and an earthquake, and Æneas Sylvius wrote home of his astonishment that in all Basle there was "nothing old or dilapidated. The church roofs shimmer with glass tiles of many colours, and many private houses have something of the same sort, so that it is a very beautiful sight to look on the city from above. The houses of the better sort are astonishingly well furnished and as finely decorated as those of Florence. They are brilliantly clean, and are for the most part painted. Sweet water gushes from ingenious fountains; and when the beauties of the town are invited by the nobles to dance, they appear in festive raiment, adorned with jewels, gold and silver, as if for the grandest wedding."

Cities, like people, should be venerated for the great moments in their past, and there is a great deal of vanished splendour in the history of Basle. The Œcumenical Council of 1424–48 was graced, not only by the visit of the Emperor Sigismund, but by the coronation of Pope Felix V; festivities both sacred and secular were organized upon a scale of luxury and abandon very unusual in Swiss history, and—a still rarer phenomenon in those parts—the women of Basle proved themselves able to satisfy the most exacting of scrutinies. Most curious are the accounts of these gaieties, in which the sophisticated formalities of the table and the dance were interrupted by the capers of "twenty-four persons disguised as wild men"; by such simple means was the balance of Nature and Artifice maintained. The fifteenth century was the great age of Basle, and our own excessive familiarity with the procedure of large international conferences should not blind us to the exceptional splendour of the feasts, balls, tournaments and night-long routs which marked the Œcumenical Council. Of the other events of the century, the Swabian and Burgundian wars can be left to the military historian; one war, to the tourist, is much like another, and the present character of the city was not as much affected by them as by the foundation, in 1460, of the University of Basle. The intensive commercial activity of the Baslers made them well able to support such a venture, and the city was already famous for the quality of its printers. The alliance of Erasmus and Amerbach well symbolizes the happy turn of events which united in one city a great centre of leaning and a great centre of book production. Three centuries later the names of Burckhardt and Nietzsche proved worthy to be set beside those of Frobenius, Erasmus, Urs Graf and Holbein. For Basle, if slow to welcome the stranger, has cobra-like powers of assimilation; when Æneas Silvius, as Pope, agreed to sanction the establishment of a University at Basle, he said that the city was "fitted above all others, by its wealth of life, its mild healthy air, and its situation on the frontiers of several nations" to be blessed with the privilege of a

86 Basle: the
Münster (*left*)

87 Rorschach: the
Kornhaus (1746-49;
*architect, G. G.
Bagnato*) (*right*)

88   The Mittelbrücke over the Rhine

89   The fifteenth-century Spalentor

BASLE

learned society; and Basle has always turned its exposed position to good account. It makes the Basler a good diplomatist; and when, as a result of some international struggle, the great lords of the earth come to Basle, and Napoleon dines at the Drei Könige, or the Tsar of Russia sends his Cossacks up the steep side of the Spalenberg, the Basler turns upon them an interested, but never an obsequious, eye. In the nineteenth century, moreover, Basle became a centre of enquiry into the nature of human effort. With Bachofen, Burckhardt and Nietzsche all solidly at work, the University of Basle could afford to look back with complacence to the illustrious epoch of the fifteenth century. Bachofen's name may not now have any general currency, but his studies of the origin of society, and more especially of primitive mythology, make this plump and affluent scholar the worthy precursor of Frazer and Malinowski. With Burckhardt we are on more familiar ground. Gifted with a quite un-Swiss facility of mind (his *Cicerone* was the result of only one year's travelling in Italy), he is known to us as a highly accomplished popularizer of difficult and complicated subjects. His books, however, were merely the debris of the brilliant extempore teaching which, from 1858 onwards, he discoursed to his students at Basle. Except for a short period when he directed the *Basler Zeitung*, Burckhardt had no experience of so-called "practical life"; it was by observation alone that he came to revise the extreme views of his youth, when he sought "only one thing—to persuade every Swiss that he is a German"; later the disorders of 1848 disposed of his hopes of living in Rome; so, with both his ideal habitations proved tenable only in an ideal past, he turned back to his home-city. Thenceforward Basle alone engaged his loyalties. "My nervous strength belongs entire", he once wrote, "to this soil . . . here, you see, my every breath can be of use." Even when, in 1872, he was invited to succeed Ranke as Professor of History at Berlin, he refused. He regarded the future, and especially the twentieth century, with a clairvoyant and unalterable pessimism. The small state was his ideal, and he viewed with dread and disgust the formation of the unified nations of German and Italy. The city-states of Greece were for him the perfect political organism; and the Swiss Confederation, though itself far from perfect, was in Burckhardt's view the only country in Europe in which true liberty was combined with political responsibility in the existence of every citizen.

It is well to prepare oneself before visiting Basle, for no city in Europe is more firmly closed to the casual visitor. In Basle nothing interesting happens out of doors or in a public place. Privately there may be any amount of acumen, intelligence and wit; but one cannot improvise an entry into Basler society, and the visitor who comes unarmed will not be put at his ease. Perambulation will be his main resource, and he will begin, like the city itself, at the Münsterplatz. This elegant square occupies, it would appear, the site of a Roman settlement. Certainly it was, at the time of the Œcumenical Council, the centre of the town. Here were held the ceremonious tourneys, of which the victor was rewarded with a fine Rhine salmon and a place in the pages of *Don Quixote*; here a Pope was crowned; and here—such is the decline in current taste—the great officials park their American cars. To-day the square is largely eighteenth century in feeling. The plain, barn-like houses are re-laxing, after the momentous events of the past; like an ancient setter before the fire, they seem almost too lazy to breathe. Here, and in the adjoining Rittergasse, the elegances of the past are frozen in ironical commentary upon the present; doors and ironwork, as is customary in Swiss cities, receive the weight of ornament which elsewhere would be distributed throughout the structure; nowhere, for instance, are there to be seen more delicate window-guards than in the Rittergasse. The Bischofshof, next the Münster, dates from the great epoch of Basle, and was built in the 1450s by Bishop Arnold von Rotberg; here, in 1473, the Emperor Friedrich III was housed during his visit to Basle. Among these trophies of the Imperial past are other houses in which the polite house-masks of the eighteenth century are discreetly combined with a workshop or ribbon-factory; the concept of the private palace is rare in Basle, and luckily the few examples of it are a triumphant success. The seventeenth century can show few buildings of interest in Basle, and the earliest good example of the big industrialist's town-house is the Ramsteinerhof, 17 Rittergasse, built in 1727–32 for Samuel Burckhardt-Zäslin, who owned both an ironworks and a salt-mine. Forty years later, when all the best places in that quarter had been taken, the brothers Sarasin picked on the Rheinsprung, five hundred yards away and next the Mittelbrücke (88), for the two palaces, the Weisse and the Blaue Haus (89), which now dominate the Rhine and complete the splendid massif of buildings, gardens and ivy-hung walls which runs from the Mittelbrücke to the Wettsteinbrücke. Even in these two palatial houses, however, the claims of commerce are not neglected, and rooms were found, in the *cours d'honneur* which give on to the Martinsgasse, for offices and workshops.

Basle is essentially a modern commercial city in which there re-main traces of a medieval town and whole stretches, each worthy of a chapter to itself, of fine houses built between 1720 and 1830. Even the classical revival is well represented—is there not a house

90   Basle : the Weisse Haus and the Blaue Haus (1763-70 ; *architect, Samuel Werenfels*)

91 St. Gall: the Abbey Church (1756-69).
Architects, G. G. Bagnato and Peter Thum

92 St. Gall: the Library (1758-67; *architect, Peter Thum;
woodwork by Anton Baumann; stucco-work by the brothers Gigl*

93 St. Gall : the Abbey Church

(22 Spitalstrasse) with Pompeian decorations on the walls?—and there are curiosities such as the Haus zum Kirschgarten, 27 Elisabethenstrasse, in which an interior of the utmost classical severity is embellished with a boudoir decorated in 1780 by Matthias Klotz, a Munich theatrical designer. But these are questions of detail; and I should fail in my duty if I did not revert to the medieval groups which remain the centre of Basler activity—the Markplatz with its Rathaus, and the red sandstone of the Münster, on its belvedere above the Rhine, with the unmolested storks secure in their nests all around. Professor Kaegi has remarked how Burckhardt grew up in the shade of the Münster and its garden, and how aptly it symbolizes his lifelong preoccupations—"built on Roman foundations, founded by a German emperor, dedicated to the cult of a Roman religion, and decorated in accordance with a meridional tradition". The original structure was burnt down in 1185, and the present building (86), so mighty in its interior design, survived the earthquake of 1356, and owes to this disaster its curious juxtaposition of Gothic and Romanesque elements. Trumpery additions of recent date cannot obscure the initial grandeur of the Münster, and still less can they affect the magnificence of its site.

Even in that privileged age when passports did not exist and one currency could be exchanged freely for another, there must have been flaws in every foreign tour—not simply the hazards of communication, although these were sometimes trying beyond anything in our experience, but also the occasions on which the travellers were too busy, or too poor, to see all that they had hoped to see. I need not attest that to-day these occasions make up a large part of our travels abroad. There is never enough money, never enough time. In preparing this book, I had always a long and shameful list of neglected churches, impenetrable German handbooks to local museums, walks abandoned in the noonday heat, unconstructive afternoons on unimportant lakes, and letters of introduction untapped in an inner pocket. And now, in writing it, I am in much the same fix. Time is up, and too much has not been said. Nothing about the Abbey of St. Maurice, so squarely erect upon a bend of the Rhône and, behind double doors, its miraculous treasure, the gathered wealth of many centuries with much to stir the imagination—from the goblet given by Haroun-al-Raschid to Charlemagne down to the valiant contributions of our own day. Nothing about Liechtenstein—a community only rivalled in its felicity by the ideal republic of the bee. Nothing about the political structure of Switzerland, or the curious anomalies which exist within it—the fact that in the very conservative canton of the Vaud, for example, the municipal council of

Lausanne has a large Socialist-Communist majority; or the heroic anti-feminism which persists throughout Switzerland. Nothing about the industrial structure of the country. Nothing about medicine or science. Nothing about the railways, or the Postautos. Nothing about the Red Cross. Nothing about the skill with which the Swiss maintain their neutrality in international relations. Nothing about the history of such great newspapers as the *Journal de Genève* and the *Gazette de Lausanne*. Nothing about the good painters whom Switzerland has fathered—Urs Graf, Paul Klee, Barthélemy Menn. Nothing about General Guisan and the regard in which he is held throughout this most peaceable of countries. Nothing about the really great museums of Switzerland. Nothing, or next to nothing, about flowers and birds. Nothing about labour problems. Too little about fish. All these are defects too large to remedy now; but a still graver offence lies in my neglect of that topmost strip of Swiss territory which includes the south bank of the Rhine between Rheinfelden and Lake Constance, the shores of that lake, the miniature highlands of Appenzell, and the memorable city of St. Gall.

Englishmen tend to think that Germans overpraise the Rhine, but even in its diminished state, along the Swiss frontier, it can exert all its famed power. Heine and Schumann may have done well to choose the Cologne reaches for the climax of *Die alten bösen Lieder*; but if we drive out from Zürich via Bülach to Eglisau, we have a first glimpse of the great river so compelling that it will at once explain its hold upon the German mind. Eglisau, a charming town in itself, is one of the few places north of the Rhine in this part of Switzerland, and one can lodge in the hotel overlooking the river, and dine on the terrace directly above its moody flood. In bad weather, in driving rain, or best of all in a thunderstorm, there is a saturnine animation in the Rhine which almost persuades one to believe that it is apart from all other rivers. Elsewhere along this stretch, the nearness of broken Germany cannot but chill the sensitive traveller, who should make haste to Schaffhausen (95). The Rhine Falls are the statutory attraction of this town; they have been so ever since the first engravers strove to reproduce the tumid scene with a calligraphic device more evocative of scrolls of false hair than of the prepotent spectacle itself. This is best seen by climbing down to the points of vantage which have been provided, kindly but not gratuitously, beneath Schloss Laufen. Even the hardened traveller will find something disturbing in the unvarying roar which can be heard from a great distance as he approaches the Falls, and in the vertiginous fascination (as of some primitive

94   Bischofszell : the Rathaus (1747-50 ; *architect, G. G. Bagnato*)

96 The Fronwagturm and Zunfthaus zur Herrenstube (1748)

95 Houses on the Vordergasse

SCHAFFHAUSEN

catastrophe) of the gigantic jets as they burst forth like living organisms from the broad surface of the upper river. But the Falls are not everything at Schaffhausen. No town in Switzerland has greater surprises to spring. An industrial town, a small river-port, the site of a Benedictine abbey, now nine centuries old, and of a sixteenth-century citadel above the Rhine, Schaffhausen is also one of the richest museums of domestic building in Switzerland. The delighted visitor will find that every period from the end of the Middle Ages to the classical style of the 1780s is represented in these exemplary streets. The painted façades of the Haus zum Ritter, the Haus zum Goldenen Ochsen and the Haus zum Riesen may have been over-restored, but one cannot but picture the effect, in earlier times, of these huge presentations of Cicero and Demosthenes, Apollo and Daphne, Ulysses and Circe, Lucretia and Dido, Paris and Helen. As for the baroque houses of Schaffhausen, they form an ensemble unsurpassed in Switzerland (96). Elsewhere, by night, such beauty is allowed to doze, remote from the daily traffic of the town; but at Schaffhausen it is the background for a night-life of surprising vivacity. Others may explain: I can only report that in this most mysterious of towns there is a profusion of little *boîtes-de-nuit*, in which are presented entertainments more appropriate to a mining-camp in some undeveloped colony than to this venerable town on the north bank of the Rhine. Most baffling is Schaffhausen; the unaccountable is so rare in Switzerland that, without wishing to pose as the Comus of tourism, I hope I may persuade others to examine this peculiar town, and to report to me upon the result of their noctambulations.

Ideally one should leave Schaffhausen before breakfast on the broad-beamed paddle-steamer which casts off for Constance at 0730 hours. Those who prefer, however, to go by road have the advantage that they can stop freely, and visit for example the island of Reichenau, so rich in memories of the exiled Buonapartes. One should supplement one's visit to the Château d'Arenenberg (given to Switzerland in 1906 by the Empress Eugénie) by perusal of the passage in which Chateaubriand described his visit to the island in August 1832. Madame Récamier had led him there from Constance, where he had been rather dull. A first reconnaissance proved favourable. The sanded paths of the property were hidden from the lake by willow-hedges, and the little pavilion frequented by the future Emperor Napoleon III stood by itself among lawns and suitable shrubs. An unseen harp, an unseen horn, agreeably affected the great prosaist as he stalked enquiringly among the grassy borders or read to Madame Récamier his description of the Gotthard. On the morrow, he dined with Queen Hortense at the château. "It is situated", he wrote, "on a sort of promontory in a chain of steep hills. The view is extensive but gloomy, and gives on to the lower lake of Constance, which is nothing but the overflowing of the Rhine among drowned meadows. On the far side one observes the dark remnants of the Black Forest, with one or two white birds swooping to and fro beneath a grey sky." The decrepitude of the little court displeased Chateaubriand, whose notes do not err on the side of charity; only in Louis Napoleon's pavilion did he find anything but futile regrets for the past, and he re-embarked with relief for the northern shore. We shall not be so particular; the pilgrimage diversifies the journey, and may be recommended. En route, the model towns of Stein-am-Rhein (85) and Diessenhofen will leave the visitor with the feeling that it was almost a pity to take them out of the box—so spotless in their enamel, so perfectly simulated the animation of their streets. In these towns we find, in its most extreme form, the tendency of Swiss houses to look newer and newer as they become older. To say this is not to be ungrateful for an exhilarating experience. Nothing could be more admirable than the civic pride which has preserved these two towns, with their many-sided oriels and scene-painted façades, in such perfect order; and nothing more simply enjoyable than the sense of colour which has turned the plainest forms of domestic architecture into a bewitchment of the eye.

The perpetual gala of Stein-am-Rhein is not reproduced in the harbours along Lake Constance. Deprived of their natural traffic with Germany and Austria, these languish; and the gloomy, greasy lake languishes with them. The baroque enthusiast should press on along these flat shores to Rorschach, near the Austrian border, where the main street, disregarded in most guide-books, yields on examination an exceptional catch of fine baroque houses, complete with heavily surmounted doors and projecting Erker. More: in the harbour itself is the Kornhaus (87) designed in 1746 by no less a man than Giovanni Gaspare Bagnato, to whom we must assign a large part of the credit for the Stiftskirche at St. Gall. Those who share my own unbridled admiration for this superb artist will bound across country to the little town of Bischofszell, where Bagnato built, between 1747 and 1750, what is without exception the finest town hall in Switzerland (94). Bischofszell is a place of small but distinct importance, and has been so since the ninth century, when its abbey was founded by the Bishop of Constance. One cannot sufficiently applaud the Providential gesture which razed a part of the town by fire in 1743, for within four years the great architect was at work and the distinguished façade was rising from the ashes. One must remark also the discernment with which the Pozzi family from Mendrisio were employed on the stucco decoration of the interior. That they should work at Einsiedeln and Solothurn was natural; but that they should post across country to a small town in Thurgau betrays great foresight on the part of somebody at Bischofszell.

I had wished to give a close account of Appenzell—to give every detail of these diminutive uplands, where the ground is never flat for more than fifty yards together, and the orchards lead directly up to the luxurious *alpages* where the cattle feast like Tudor monarchs; where peasant costume is still an affair of ribbons and velvet, and where unnamed artists have left such memorable pictures of the simple richness of their existence. If I do not describe all this, and the wooden chalets in which each storey overhangs the one below it, it is because I have not been there long enough and cannot trust myself to be accurate. Besides, I have always intended to close this book with an account of St. Gall.

St. Gall is not only a town of great distinction, it is the town to which, early in the seventh century, came the first and most influential of visitors from the British Isles. St. Columba was an Irish monk, and his pupil, the hermit St. Gall, gave his name to the abbey of which the first ground-plan, dated about A.D. 820, still exists in the abbey library. Of the various buildings which housed the abbey and its servants during the following nine hundred years, little trace now remains. There is nothing to compare with the eighth-century circular crypt at St. Maurice, or the Merovingian crypt at Disentis. All the present buildings at St. Gall—the abbey itself dating from 1755 to 1769, and the rectangular block of office buildings from nearly a century earlier—are post-Renaissance. The church is, with Einsiedeln, the greatest single monument in Switzerland. Where Einsiedeln stands alone, like a cliff with a dead sea of architectural rubbish at its foot, St. Gall fits with perfect neatness into a prosperous and original town (93). There is no wasted ground in St. Gall. The town does not straggle; as at Berne, one can stand in its centre and yet see, at the end of each perspective, green all around one; and it is a town in which the future matters as much as the past. There is none of the expiring sweetness of the *ville d'art* in St. Gall; it lives in, but not on, the achievement of the past—the Erkers in which caryatides support the swelling balconies, each adorned with symbols of mythology or of the magical resources of some distant country; the square-faced Bürgerhäuser of the sixteenth century; the "Kleine Engelberg" in the Marktgasse (3), one of the loveliest façades in the country; the Karlstor, which marked in 1570 the limit of the *enceinte*; and even, one must suppose, the house, 76 Dufourstrasse, which Dr. Jenny describes as "English country-house Gothic, 1901–5". It is the sense of drive which makes St. Gall an exhilarating town even for those who detest baroque monuments. Those who like them may be assured that this church (2, 93) is the peer of Einsiedeln, and that, as a painter and *stuccatore*, Christian Wenzinger can compare very well with the Asams. The proud name of J. A. Feuchtmayr recurs, moreover, in connection with the choir-stalls and the confessional-boxes. For all one's loyalty to Bagnato, it is possible to rejoice that his projected galleries were not carried out, and that the prime effect of the church is now one of expansive freedom and aerial lightness, as the eye scampers across Wenzinger's uncrowded rotunda and up away into the choir (91). This is a radiant, audacious creation, remote as Einsiedeln from the darkly reverberant fanes of the North. There is much to admire, too, in the placing of the church against the martial sobriety of the former abbey buildings. I do not know when it is the more wonderful—in summer, when the lawns show up the delicate colour, and the as delicate moulding and recession, of the exterior of the church, or in winter, when white calls to white across the snowy floor of the square, and the brilliance of the icy crystals at one's feet is answered and exceeded by the brilliance of the great building which Man has erected to mark his adoration. As we slide round the abbey library (92) in our cloth overshoes, there is more at which to marvel, for in this small but miraculous sanctum the brothers Gigl, who also worked in the stucco decoration of the Stiftskirche, have played off their art against the sunbrowned walnut of the walls and floor. In their wire cages the great folios, the rare text of Seneca and the manuscript of Virgil, sit side by side with English classics of theology and law. This welcoming room in a thriving and beautiful town, itself surrounded by a landscape of Elysian simplicity—it is for such things that I, for one, like most to remember Switzerland.

Index

Entries in Italics refer to individuals; other entries to places. References in heavy type are to figure numbers of illustrations.